CW01021600

Indian

MADE EASY

Indian

MADE EASY

AMANDIP UPPAL

PHOTOGRAPHS BY LISA LINDER

MURDOCH BOOKS

SYDNEY · LONDON

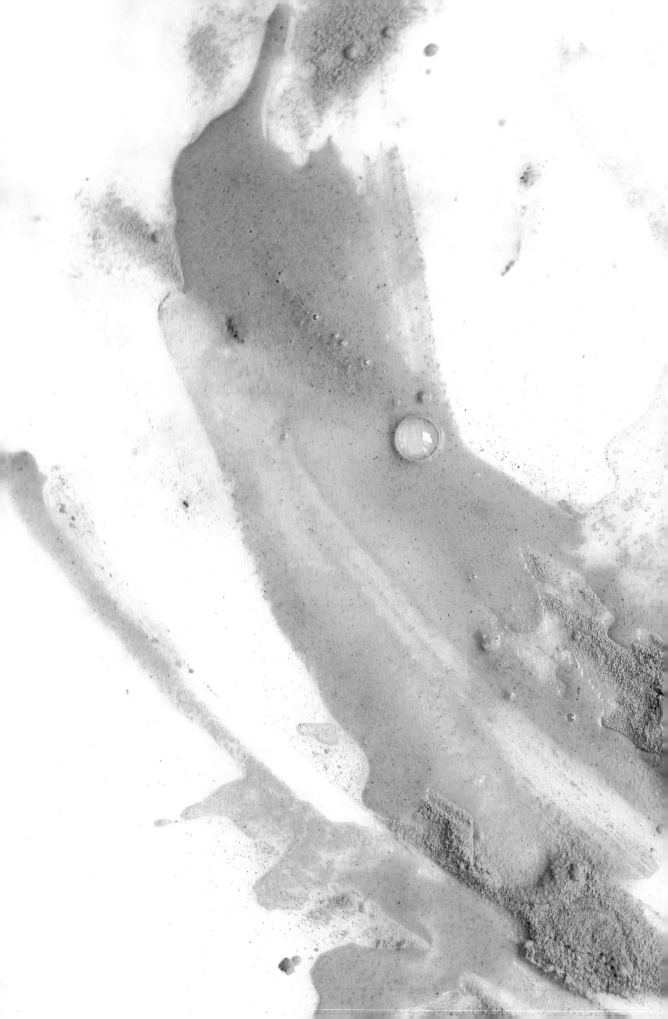

Contents

This book is about discovering a *casual* attitude towards Indian cookery, provoking the inventive side in experienced cooks and building confidence in others. This is a book that you reach out for, one that provides familiarity and comfort, and one for everyday use whatever the occasion may be.

Stripped back are the regal layers associated with Indian cuisine, making way for a new casual approach to cooking with Indian spices and ingredients. In this book you will find traditional favourites plus classic dishes from the north and south of India, some of which have been distilled and pared back for busy modern cooks. The recipes continue to hold true to tradition while fitting in with the way you want to cook – preparing ahead where possible and making shopping easy.

Indian Made Easy brings Indian cookery *up to date*, and will provide you with the basics and inspiration to forge your own path and try something new. Recipes such as Lemon and Saffron Pot Roast Chicken, Baked Salmon with Crème Fraîche and Coconut or Chilli Hot Chocolate will warm the soul, fire up a love for food and build an appreciation of spices you may have never even heard of. These are recipes to celebrate and share communally.

Quick, uncomplicated dishes, with simple steps and helpful tips, will allow you to dip in and out of Indian cooking as and when the mood suits you. It is all about cooking with ease, organisation and simplicity, and guiding you along the way until eventually you feel confident and inspired to use spices in more ways than one.

The love and *appreciation* of good food is a common thread that runs through all the regions of India, central to family life, culture and pleasure. *Indian Made Easy* invites you to join in the experience.

Stars of India

INDIA IS FAMOUS FOR MANY EXCITING REASONS: THE PEOPLE, SPIRITUALITY, AND OF COURSE BOLLYWOOD … BUT THE MAIN PULSE AND HEART OF INDIA IS THE FOOD.

DALAI LAMA
His holiness the 14th Dalai Lama
From: Himachal Pradesh
Famous Dishes: Dham, Patande

MAHATMA GANDHI
'Father of the Nation'
From: Gujarat
Famous Dishes: Dhokla, Coriander and Peanut Chutney, Shrikand

DEEPAK CHOPRA
New Age guru and advocate of alternative medicine
From: Delhi
Famous Dishes: Butter Chicken, Kulfi

FREDDIE MERCURY
Flamboyant and eccentric rock star
From: Maharashtra
Famous Dishes: Pav Bhaji, Flaked Rice Poha

RAVI SHANKAR
World famous classical sitar player and composer
From: Uttar Pradesh
Famous Dishes: Peda, Bharwan Chicken

ENGELBERT HUMPERDINCK
An English pop singer and heart-throb
From: Tamil Nadu
Famous Dishes: Idli Sambhar, Masala Dosa

GEORGE ORWELL
Political writer, journalist and novelist
From: Bengal
Famous Dishes: Ilish Paturi, Ras Malai

MIRA NAIR
Accomplished film director/writer/producer
From: Orissa
Famous Dishes: Crab Kalia, Stuffed Okra

FREIDA PINTO
Most famous for *Slumdog Millionaire* and *Rise of the Planet of the Apes*
From: Goa
Famous Dishes: Prawn Curry, Spicy Sausages

ANUPAM KHER
Mainly a Bollywood actor who has appeared in several hundred films
From: Kashmir
Famous Dishes: Dum Aloo, Yoghurt Lamb Curry

AISHWARYA RAI BACHCHAN
Former Miss World model turned Indian actress
From: Karnataka
Famous Dishes: Beetroot Curry, Lemon Rice

OM PURI
An Indian actor who has appeared in mainstream commercial Indian and British films
From: Punjab
Famous Dishes: Dhal Makhani, Chicken and Paneer Tikka

KASHMIR
Dum Aloo

HIMACHAL PRADESH
Patande

PUNJAB
Dhal Makhani

DELHI
Kulfi

GUJARAT
Coriander and Peanut Chutney

BENGAL
Ilish Paturi

MAHARASHTRA
Pav Bhaji

UTTAR PRADESH
Peda

ORISSA
Stuffed Okra

KARNATAKA
Lemon Rice

GOA
Spicy Sausages

TAMIL NADU
Idli Sambhar

Pantry / Larder

WHOLE SPICES

Each pungent and aromatic spice can hold its own or they can be mixed and matched to create your own unique blends of masala.

FENNEL SEEDS

Fennel has an aniseed flavour that gives a warm, sweet aroma.

CINNAMON STICKS

Cinnamon sticks produce a slightly spicy, sweet flavour. Use ground cinnamon for extra flavour and deep colour. As an alternative, cassia, which comes from cassia bark, is related to 'true cinnamon'.

CLOVES

Cloves can be used whole or ground for a powerful sweet, but peppery flavour.

NIGELLA SEEDS

Ideally used whole in pickles, curries, breads and salads, these seeds can be toasted and ground at home.

BLACK CARDAMOM

The aroma and flavour of black cardamom is quite different from small cardamom. It has a distinct smoky, minty coolness to its flavour.

GREEN CARDAMOM

Second to black pepper, cardamom is one of the most popular spices in the world. It works beautifully in milky desserts or savoury curries.

FENUGREEK SEEDS

This small hard seed has a tangy, burnt-sugar flavour, so only use in small quantities.

BAY LEAVES

These leaves are frequently used in rice and meat dishes, but are also delicious in dhals and vegetables.

MUSTARD SEEDS

Mustard seeds come in three colours: yellow, brown and black. It's the black ones that are most commonly used in Indian cooking, and are only used in dhals, pickles, salad dressings and chutneys – almost never in meat dishes.

BLACK PEPPERCORNS

The perfect spice and seasoning used in every type of regional cooking – use black peppercorns whole or crushed in meat, vegetable, lentil and rice dishes.

WHOLE CUMIN SEEDS

This spice is often used whole and added to hot oil or can be ground. For a smoky, earthy flavour toast the seeds first and then grind.

WHOLE CORIANDER SEEDS

These little lemony, sweet balls can be ground, toasted, crushed or used whole. They are ideal in pickles or ground in curry pastes.

COCONUT MILK POWDER

CUMIN SEEDS

CINNAMON STICKS

TURMERIC

CARDAMOM PODS

STAR ANISE

AJWAIN (CAROM) SEED

Also known as lovage, this seed certainly has a distinct, piquant flavour. It is mainly used in vegetables, pickles and breads.

CARAWAY SEEDS

This versatile seed releases a very aromatic, sharp and nutty flavour. Add to bread, meat and fish dishes for extra character.

FENUGREEK LEAVES

Known as kasuri methi, these dried leaves add a strong, distinctive flavour to a curry. Rub the leaves between your fingers while adding to your dish to release the flavour.

MACE AND NUTMEG

Both these spices are formed on the same plant, they are quite similar in flavour and are mostly used in meat curries and desserts.

WHITE POPPY SEEDS

These add richness to a dish. They can be roasted, ground and then added to dishes or soaked in hot water and made into a thick paste.

PANCH PHORAN

Also known as Bengali five spice, they are used to infuse the oil and add wonderful layers of flavour to most dishes. Ready-mixed packets of these seeds are available to buy, but if you can't find them then mix together equal quantities of fenugreek seeds (methi dana), cumin seeds (jeera), aniseed (saunf), black mustard seeds (rai) and onion seeds (kalonji). Store the mix in an airtight jar and use as and when it is needed.

GROUND SPICES

Ideally, try and buy ground spices in small quantities and store in screw-top jars or containers.

TURMERIC

Not only does this spice add a beautiful deep rich colour to your dishes, turmeric is also a powerful antioxidant, and so is great for digestion and healing.

CHILLI POWDER AND FLAKES

Chilli is an important spice, as it gives a dish that bold blend of heat, fragrance and flavour. Both equally as hot, but flecks of red chilli flakes look attractive, while the powder is best used during cooking as it also releases colour. For a deeper colour Kashmiri chilli powder works best. If ground or fresh chillies are too hot for you, then replace with cayenne or freshly ground black pepper.

GARAM MASALA

Every region, and even each household, in India has their own version of garam masala. A maximum of seven whole spices blended together feature in most curries for that aromatic warmth. Shop-bought powder is fine, but making your own is also easy (see page 242).

TANDOORI MASALA

A mixture of ground spices specifically used for tandoors, or clay oven skewered meats and vegetable dishes. Firm favourites include, tikka, butter chicken or paneer as an alternative.

SAFFRON

CORIANDER SEEDS

MACE FLOWERS

BAY LEAVES

CHILLI FLAKES

GARAM MASALA

KIDNEY BEANS

RAW COCONUT OIL

WHITE RICE

1/2 TEASPOON

1/4 TEASPOON

MUSTARD OIL

CHICKPEAS

GHEE

OILS AND BUTTER

MUSTARD SEED OIL

This oil is a popular one for cooking fish in particular and as a base for pickles. It also has a high cooking point, so perfect for deep-frying. **Note:** Heat this oil until a little smoky, cool slightly and then use.

GROUNDNUT OIL

An excellent all-purpose oil that is light and extremely popular in most Asian cuisines.

GHEE

An Indian version of clarified butter, ghee has a high burning point and tastes divine in dishes (see page 234). If ghee is too rich to cook with, then finish off your dish with a drizzle of this yellow, nutty liquid.

COCONUT OIL

Another oil that has a high burning point, and is classified as a 'superfood' that has amazing health benefits and is delicious. Organic raw virgin coconut oil is best.

ESSENCE AND FLAVOURING

CHAAT MASALA

This is a zingy, tangy and slightly hot masala, which is mainly used as a garnish on salads, snacks, drinks and sometimes curries.

BLACK SALT

Known as Kala Namak, this salt has a pinkish colour, but once added to salads, chopped fruits and curries it adds a distinct flavour.

KEWRA WATER

An extract from the pandanus flower, it is mainly used in meat dishes, rice dishes, drinks and desserts and is similar to rosewater.

ROSEWATER

This is a scented water made with rose petals and is delicious used in desserts, drinks and savoury rice dishes.

SAFFRON

Saffron is an expensive, delicately flavoured spice that has an exquisite taste and colour. Soak the fine threads in warm milk, water or stock and add to sweet or savoury dishes and drinks.

COCONUT MILK POWDER

A perfect all-rounder for adding a smooth richness to curries, soups, dressings, marinades and cakes. Unless using in baking, make sure to mix with a little warm water to form a paste before adding.

COCONUT MILK

Fairly similar result as to the coconut milk powder, just saucier. Coconut milk is great for using in broths, marinades and gravy-based curries.

DRY MANGO POWDER (AMCHOOR)

This sour powder is made from dried green mangoes. It is used mainly in vegetable and bean dishes to add that edge of fruity sourness. If you can't find dry mango powder then use lemon or lime juice instead.

POMEGRANATE SEED POWDER (ANARDHANA)

This powder has a tart and tangy flavour, and is used mostly in crispy fritters, fried snacks, chutneys, yoghurts and sometimes curries.

DRY GOODS

SEV

Crispy fine noodles made from chickpea flour (besan) – you can sprinkle them on most snack dishes, or enjoy them on their own served with drinks.

PUFFED RICE

Usually used in breakfast cereals, snack foods and popular street foods in India.

DRIED MINT

For a further intense minty flavour, add to marinades, dressings, spice mixes and stuffings.

BEANS AND LENTILS

Beans and lentils have an advantage of adding bulk to a dish or salad and they are also a great substitute for a meat-free meal. **Note:** The longer you cook beans and lentils over a low heat and stir, the richer and creamier the texture becomes.

PUY LENTILS

Not traditionally used in Indian cooking, however with their lovely bite, and flavour, Puy lentils blend very well with other spices. They are delicious cooked in stock and whole spices and used in salads, mixed into a vegetable curry or scattered over rice with a crispy onion garnish.

MOONG DHAL

This is a skinned yellow split moong bean. It's very quick to cook and is also delicious as a dry-fried dhal.

MASOOR DHAL

A wonderful and versatile lentil that is happy to be blended with other quick-cook lentils. It can be used on its own as a simple dhal or to bulk up most soups.

URAD DHAL

Also know as black gram, these have a distinct strong earthy taste. They are traditionally used in curries, but also ground into a flour or paste and used to make poppadoms and dosas. **Note:** This lentil needs to be soaked overnight before using, but good-quality, cooked varieties are also available in tins or cartons.

TOOR DHAL

Toor dhal has a unique, mild nutty flavour. Cook it as a soupy broth or mix in with moong dhal and masoor dhal for more variety in flavour and texture.

KIDNEY BEANS

This creamy, buttery bean works very well mixed in and cooked with most lentil, vegetable and meat dishes. **Note:** This legume needs to be soaked overnight before using, but good-quality, cooked varieties are also available in tins or cartons.

CHICKPEAS

Chickpeas have endless uses, but are mainly added to salads, vegetable curries, rice and meat dishes. **Note:** This legume needs to be soaked overnight before using, but good-quality, cooked varieties are also available in tins or cartons.

FREEZER ESSENTIALS

CURRY LEAVES

Buy a large batch of these leaves fresh and freeze. Similar to a bay leaf, only smaller, they release a distinct taste and aroma and are added to rice, curries, chutneys, salads and pickles. Alternatively, you can use bay leaves.

FRESH GRATED COCONUT

Buy several fresh coconuts, scrape out the flesh and freeze in individual freezer-proof bags.

TAMARIND PULP

Although you can buy jars of tamarind pulp, making your own is very easy and much tastier (see page 228). It can be stored in the refrigerator, but it also freezes very well.

CURRY LEAVES

TAMARIND PULP

MOONG DHAL

GHEE

CHICKPEA FLOUR (BESAN)

15 Must-have Spices

START BUILDING YOUR BASIC 'SPICE SHELF' WITH THESE 15 CRUCIAL
AND MOST COMMONLY USED SPICES. REGULARLY FEATURED,
SO THEY ARE GUARANTEED TO BE USED OVER AND OVER AGAIN.

1 TURMERIC

Ayurvedic Jamu Tonic Drink p.214

Beef and Potato Curry p.110

Cauliflower and Peas p.68

Classic Lamb Curry p.100

Crab-fried Rice p.148

South Indian Eggplant Pickle p.184

Tarka Dhal with Spinach and Fresh Tomato p.60

2 RED CHILLI FLAKES/POWDER OR CAYENNE

Bean and Lentil Salad with Garlic and Ginger p.168

Eggplant with Chilli and Pomegranate Dressing p.86

Kale, Chickpea, Mint and Preserved Lemon Salad p.162

Parantha with Ajwain, Fennel and Chilli Butter p.120

Stuffed Okra p.80

3 GARAM MASALA

Chicken Pulao p.152

Classic Lamb Curry p.100

Crab-fried Rice p.148

Kidney Beans and Potatoes p.78

Lamb Kofta and Saffron Crème Fraîche p.106

Lamb Biryani p.154

Mussels in Chilli, Ginger and Curry Leaf Broth p.96

4 CUMIN SEEDS

Ayurvedic Detox Tea p.220

Kale, Chickpea, Mint and Preserved Lemon Salad p.162

Khichadi p.136

Kidney Beans and Potato p.78

Lamb Biryani p.154

Lemon and Chickpea Rice p.146

South Indian Eggplant Pickle p.184

Tarka Dhal with Spinach and Fresh Tomato p.60

5 GROUND CUMIN

Bean and Lentil Salad with Garlic and Ginger p.168

Classic Lamb Curry p.100

Lemon and Saffron Pot Roast Chicken p.102

Masala Roast Lamb p.94

Squid with Shallots, Ginger and Chilli p.92

Stuffed Okra p.80

6 CORIANDER SEEDS

Ayurvedic Detox Tea p.220

Basic Spiced Tomato Paste p.237

Cauliflower and Peas p.68

Lamb and Apricot Pasties p.32

Potato and Pea Samosas p.50

7
GROUND CORIANDER

Bean and Lentil Salad with Garlic and Ginger p.168

Chicken Korma p.98

Classic Lamb Curry p.100

Lamb Cutlets in Spiced Breadcrumbs p.30

Masala Roast Lamb p.94

Stuffed Potato and Pea Cakes p.156

8
BLACK MUSTARD SEEDS

Beetroot Curry p.76

Garlic, Ginger and Chilli Prawns p.38

Lemon and Chickpea Rice p.146

Mumbai Aloo p.156

South Indian Eggplant Pickle p.184

9
CASSIA OR CINNAMON STICKS

Ayurvedic Detox Tea p.220

Beef and Potato Curry p.110

Chana Masala p.58

Chicken Pulao p.152

Fish, Green Beans and Spinach Kedgeree p.22

Lamb Biryani p.154

10
BAY LEAVES

Beef and Potato Curry p.110

Chicken Korma p.98

Chicken Pulao p.152

Lamb Biryani p.154

Lemon and Saffron Pot Roast Chicken p.102

11
GREEN CARDAMOM

Cardamom Coffee p.218

Chicken Korma p.98

Chicken Pulao p.152

Coconut Rice p.138

Lamb Biryani p.154

Masala Chai p.212

Carrot and Orange Balls with Chocolate p.204

12
SAFFRON

Lamb Biryani p.154

Lamb Kofta and Saffron Crème Fraîche p.106

Lemon and Saffron Pot Roast Chicken p.102

Pistachio Kulfi p.200

Saffron and Cashew Rice p.150

13
COCONUT MILK POWDER

Baked Salmon with Crème Fraîche and Coconut p.104

Butter Chicken p.114

Creamy Peas and Mushrooms p.64

Fresh Tomato and Curry Leaf p.88

Mussels in Chilli, Ginger and Curry Leaf Broth p.96

Spiced Coconut and Crème Fraîche Marinade p.246

14
CURRY LEAVES

Beetroot Curry p.76

Coconut Rice p.138

Fish in Tamarind Sauce p.108

Flaked Rice and Mixed Nut Poha p.24

Fresh Tomato and Curry Leaf p.88

Mussels in Chilli, Ginger and Curry Leaf Broth p.96

Shallots with Tamarind and Toasted Coconut p.62

15
TAMARIND PULP

Crab-fried Rice p.148

Fish in Tamarind Sauce p.108

Fresh Tomato, Date and Tamarind Relish p.176

Fruit Chutney p.186

Shallots with Tamarind and Toasted Coconut p.62

Tamarind Rice p.144

Light
Bites

CHAPTER 1

Fish, Green Beans and Spinach Kedgeree

THIS IS A DELICIOUS AND RICH TAKE ON THE TRADITIONAL KEDGEREE RECIPE. IF YOU DON'T EAT FISH, TRY THIS WITH A SPRINKLE OF SMOKED PAPRIKA FOR A SMOKY EDGE AND ENJOY AS A VEGETARIAN OPTION.

SERVES 2 | PREPARATION TIME: 20 MINUTES | COOKING TIME: 15 MINUTES

FRESH

500g undyed smoked haddock

¼ leek or onion, finely chopped

2 garlic cloves, very finely chopped

1 quantity cooked Simple Plain Rice (see page 134)

100g green beans, halved

20–25ml light (single) cream

200g spinach, stalks removed, leaves roughly chopped

grated zest of 1 lemon

3 boiled eggs, quartered

SPICES

2.5cm piece cassia or cinnamon stick

2 bay leaves

1 teaspoon fennel seeds

¼ teaspoon ground turmeric

¼ teaspoon red chilli flakes

PANTRY/LARDER

1 tablespoon butter or oil

50–70ml vegetable or fish stock

salt, to taste (optional)

1. Bring about 300ml water to the boil in a large shallow pan. Add the smoked haddock and simmer for 4 minutes, or until the fish is just cooked. Lift it out onto a plate and leave until cool enough to handle.

2. Heat the butter or oil in a large frying pan over a low–medium heat. Add the cassia or cinnamon stick, bay leaves, leek or onion, garlic and fennel seeds and fry until lightly browned. Reduce the heat slightly, add the turmeric, chilli flakes and green beans and fry for 20 seconds.

3. Next, turn up the heat slightly and pour in the stock. Bring to a gentle simmer and cook for 4–5 minutes, or until the beans are al dente and the stock has reduced. Stir in the cream and cook gently for 1–2 minutes, then gently stir in the spinach and salt, if using. Turn off the heat; mix in the flaked haddock and lemon zest and combine with the cooked rice. Serve garnished with the quartered boiled eggs.

Flaked Rice and Mixed Nut Poha

THIS DISH IS LIGHT, YET FILLING AND IS A FIRM FAVOURITE FOR BRUNCH IN INDIA, TRADITIONALLY SERVED ALONGSIDE AN ARRAY OF CHUTNEYS AND PICKLES. IT CAN ALSO BE EATEN ON ITS OWN OR AS AN ACCOMPANIMENT TO GRILLED OR BARBECUED FISH OR MEAT.

SERVES 3–4 | PREPARATION TIME: 45 MINUTES | COOKING TIME: 15 MINUTES

FRESH
10–12 fresh curry leaves

½ onion, finely chopped

2 medium potatoes, boiled with skin on, cooled and cubed

1 green chilli, thinly sliced (optional)

3 tablespoons finely chopped coriander

4 lemon wedges

SPICES
1 generous pinch of asafoetida

½ teaspoon mustard seeds

½ teaspoon whole cumin seeds

1 dried chilli

¼ teaspoon ground turmeric

PANTRY/LARDER
140g poha rice (dry flaked rice)

3 tablespoons oil

1 teaspoon salt, or to taste

½ teaspoon sugar

2 tablespoons roasted peanuts, roughly chopped

1. Rinse the poha in a sieve gently but thoroughly under cold running water. Empty into a bowl, cover generously with fresh water and leave to soak for about 5 minutes. Drain and leave in the sieve set over a bowl.

2. Heat the oil in a large non-stick frying pan over a medium–high heat. After 2 minutes, add the asafoetida, then reduce the heat slightly and keep stirring for 2 minutes. Add the mustard seeds, cumin seeds and dried chilli and fry for a further 1 minute.

3. Immediately toss in the curry leaves, turmeric and salt. Add the onion and fry for 2–3 minutes until golden brown. Add the potatoes and sliced chilli, if using, and continue to fry for a further 2 minutes, or until slightly brown.

4. Add the sugar, reduce the heat to low and add the poha. Stir gently, while making sure everything is mixed together and keep tossing thoroughly for 3–4 minutes. Turn off the heat, stir in the coriander and peanuts and squeeze over the lemon wedges. Serve hot or at room temperature.

Carrot and Chickpea Pancakes

THESE QUICK, WHEAT-FREE PANCAKES ARE PERFECT FOR ANY TIME OF THE DAY AND CAN BE ENJOYED HOT OR COLD. STUFF THEM WITH MUMBAI ALOO (SEE PAGE 156) AND A DRIZZLE OF GARLIC AND RED CHILLI CHUTNEY (SEE PAGE 178) TO MAKE A FILLING MEAL.

SERVES 2 | PREPARATION TIME: 30 MINUTES | COOKING TIME: ABOUT 4 MINUTES

FRESH
5cm piece ginger, peeled and finely chopped

2 spring onions, finely chopped

1 carrot, grated

1 green chilli, seeded (optional) and finely chopped, or large pinch of red chilli flakes

1 tablespoon finely chopped coriander

SPICES
¼ teaspoon ajwain seeds

¼ teaspoon ground cumin

PANTRY/LARDER
½ teaspoon salt, or to taste

125g fine chickpea flour (besan)

1–2 tablespoons ghee or oil

1. Place all the ingredients, except the ghee or oil into a large bowl and mix, gradually adding 80–100ml cold water, until the batter mix resembles the consistency of double cream.

2. Dip some paper towel into the ghee or oil and carefully wipe the inside of a non-stick crêpe or frying pan to coat the entire pan. Heat the pan over a medium heat, then gradually pour in one ladleful of the batter and swirl the pan to get a nice even layer.

3. Cook for about 35–40 seconds, then gently lift out with a palette knife to check if it is golden brown. Flip over and cook the other side for about 35–40 seconds. Continue this process until all the batter is finished. Serve.

Vegetable Parantha Rolls

THESE HAND-HELD WRAPS ARE GREAT PICNIC FOOD AND CAN BE A FUN WAY TO INTRODUCE SPICES TO KIDS — JUST OMIT THE CHILLIES IF YOU LIKE. ADD SALAD LEAVES OR A SPOONFUL OF RAW MANGO, APPLE CORIANDER AND MINT RELISH (SEE PAGE 174). PARANTHAS ARE EASY TO MAKE, BUT FLATBREADS ARE JUST AS GOOD IF YOU ARE SHORT OF TIME.

SERVES 6–8 | PREPARATION TIME: 25 MINUTES | COOKING TIME: 5 MINUTES

FRESH
170g potatoes, peeled and cut into cubes
230g carrots, cubed
110g peas
2.5cm piece ginger, peeled and finely shredded
1 tablespoon finely chopped coriander
1 green chilli, finely chopped

SPICES
1 teaspoon cumin seeds
2 teaspoons fenugreek leaves
½ teaspoon ground turmeric
1 teaspoon garam masala

PANTRY/LARDER
2 tablespoons oil
salt, to taste
1 teaspoon ghee, to drizzle
4 plain flaky Paranthas (see note, page 120)

1. Boil the potatoes and carrots for 4–5 minutes until almost tender. Add the peas and simmer for a few minutes more, then drain.

2. Heat the oil in a frying pan over a low–medium heat. Add the cumin seeds and fry for 10 seconds. Next, add all the parboiled vegetables, ginger, green chilli, fenugreek leaves and salt and stir-fry for 30 seconds. Add the turmeric and garam masala and fry for a further 1 minute, then add the coriander. Turn the heat right down, place a lid on top and cook for a further 2–3 minutes, or until the vegetables are completely cooked through.

3. Take off the heat, drizzle with ghee and slightly mash the vegetables with a fork. Cool slightly and serve in the middle of a parantha. Serve either open or as a wrap.

Lamb Cutlets in Spiced Breadcrumbs

RUSTIC AND LUXURIOUS ALL AT ONCE, THESE LAMB CUTLETS
MAKE A HEAVENLY CANAPÉ OR SPECIAL START TO A MEAL.
TAKE CARE NOT TO OVERCOOK THE LAMB — IT SHOULD BE
TENDER AND PINK WITHIN THE CRISP SPICED CRUMB.

SERVES 4 | PREPARATION TIME: 30 MINUTES
MARINATING TIME: 1–8 HOURS | COOKING TIME: 15 MINUTES

FRESH

10 lamb cutlets, French trimmed

2 garlic cloves, very finely chopped

1cm piece ginger, peeled and finely grated

2 green chillies, finely chopped

100g breadcrumbs, made from stale bread

2 eggs

grated zest of 1 lemon

2 tablespoons finely chopped coriander

SPICES

2 teaspoons ground cumin

2 teaspoons ground coriander

2 teaspoons garam masala

PANTRY/LARDER

2 tablespoons oil, plus extra for shallow-frying

30g plain flour

½ teaspoon salt, or to taste

1. Use your hands to flatten each cutlet, then place in a large bowl and massage in the garlic, ginger, chillies, ground cumin, ground coriander and the 2 tablespoons oil. Cover with plastic wrap and chill for at least 1 hour, or preferably overnight.

2. Remove the lamb cutlets from the refrigerator and allow to come up to room temperature. Mix the breadcrumbs with the lemon zest, fresh coriander, garam masala and salt.

3. Next, whisk the eggs in a bowl. Then, mix the flour with the salt and spread on a plate. Spread the spiced breadcrumbs out on another plate.

4. Take 1 lamb cutlet at a time, coat in the flour, shaking off excess, then dip in the egg, and finally, coat in the spiced breadcrumbs. Place on a tray and repeat with the remaining cutlets.

5. Heat enough oil in a large frying pan for shallow-frying over a medium heat. Cook the cutlets, in batches, for 3 minutes on each side for medium.

Lamb and Apricot Pasties

THESE LITTLE PASTIES ARE PACKED WITH DELICATE SWEET AND SPICY FLAVOURS. FOR AN AUTHENTIC RESULT, THE PASTRY IS WELL WORTH ATTEMPTING, BUT TO CUT PREP TIME YOU CAN ALSO USE FILO PASTRY FOR FRYING OR SHORTCRUST PASTRY FOR BAKING.

MAKES ABOUT 20 | PREPARATION TIME: 45 MINUTES | COOKING TIME: 1 HOUR

FRESH

500g lamb mince

½ small onion, finely chopped

1 garlic clove, crushed

1cm piece ginger, peeled and grated or finely chopped

1 green chilli, finely chopped

2 tablespoons finely chopped coriander or mint

1 quantity Rich Indian Pastry (see page 250)

SPICES

Four Whole Spice Bouquet Garni (see page 248)

1½ teaspoons cumin seeds

1½ teaspoons coriander seeds

1½ teaspoons garam masala

PANTRY/LARDER

30g dried apricots, finely diced

½–1 teaspoon salt, or to taste

2 tablespoons plain flour

1.5 litres oil

1. In a heavy-based saucepan, place the mince, bouquet garni, cumin seeds and coriander seeds.

2. Pour cold water into the pan until it reaches 1cm above the mince. Bring to the boil and boil over a medium heat for about 40 minutes, stirring occasionally.

3. Add the onion, garlic, ginger, chilli, apricots, garam masala and salt. Reduce the heat to low and simmer, stirring occasionally, for a further 15 minutes, or until the moisture has completely dried out. Cool to room temperature, remove the bouquet garni, then stir in the coriander or mint.

4. Mix together the plain flour and 1 tablespoon water to make a sticky glue and set aside.

5. Divide the dough in half, roll out quite thinly and, using a 10cm cutter, cut out 9–10 circles. Repeat with the second half of the dough.

6. Place 1 tablespoon of filling in the middle of each circle, dip your finger into the sticky flour glue and run your finger around the edge of each pastry circle.

7. Fold the Indian Pastry dough over to form a semi-circle shape, then carefully pinch and seal all around the edge. Repeat until all the ingredients are used.

8. Heat the oil in a saucepan over a medium heat. Fry the pasties 4 at a time for 3–4 minutes, or until the pastry is golden brown. Drain on paper towel and serve hot or cold.

NOTE: Double-fry the pasties for a crispier pastry.

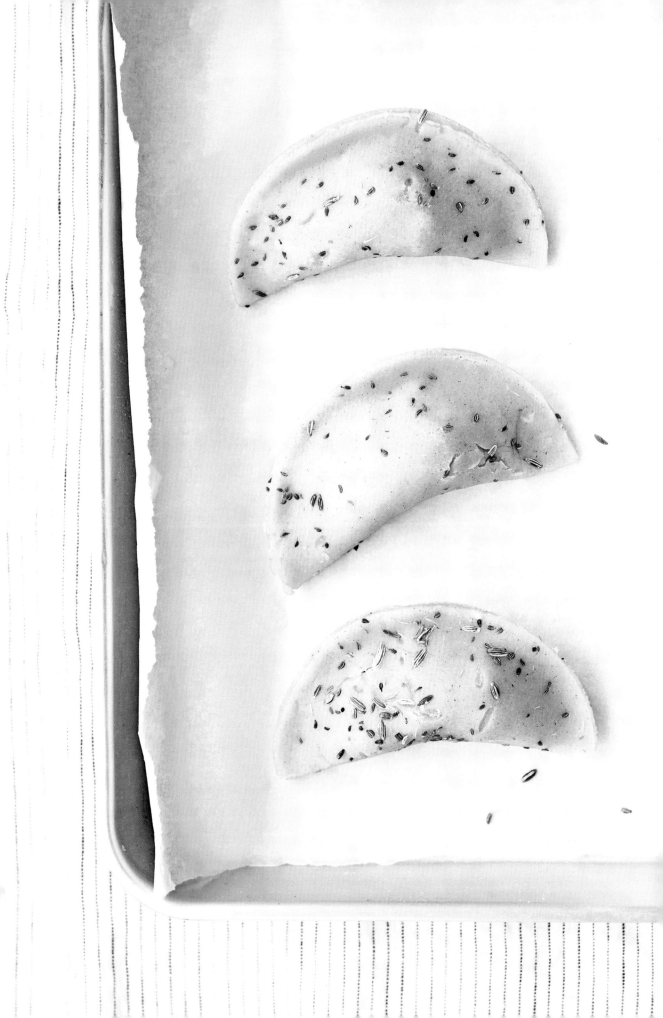

Fish Fritters

IF YOU LOVE BOTH FISH AND CHIPS AND SPICY FOOD, THIS RECIPE
MAKES FOR A PERFECT COMBINATION. THE BATTER IS A LIGHTER
ADAPTATION OF A CLASSIC PAKORA COATING AND IS MADE WITH
SPARKLING WATER AND EGGS. SERVE WITH MAYONNAISE, A SQUEEZE OF
LIME AND A HANDFUL OF SHREDDED CORIANDER STIRRED THROUGH, OR
SOME FRESH TOMATO, DATE AND TAMARIND RELISH (SEE PAGE 176).

SERVES 2–4 | PREPARATION TIME: 35 MINUTES
MARINATING TIME: 10–15 MINUTES | COOKING TIME: 25 MINUTES

FRESH

500g firm white fish eg haddock
or cod, cut into medium goujons

juice of 1 lime

2 eggs

SPICES

¼ teaspoon chilli powder

¼ teaspoon ajwain seeds

½ teaspoon ground cumin

½ teaspoon ground coriander

1 teaspoon tandoori masala

PANTRY/LARDER

¼ teaspoon salt, plus extra to taste

150ml ice-cold sparkling water

115g plain flour

55g cornflour

oil, for deep-frying

GARNISH

½ lime

1 spring onion, cut into julienne

2 teaspoons chaat masala
or sea salt (optional)

1. Place the fish pieces in a shallow dish and add the salt, chilli powder and lime juice. Cover with plastic wrap and refrigerate for 10–15 minutes.

2. Whisk the eggs in a large, deep bowl, then pour in the sparkling water and mix quickly. Next, add the flours, ajwain seeds, ground cumin, ground coriander, tandoori masala and salt to taste. Stir gently with a fork, making sure not to overmix. The batter should have lumps.

3. Heat enough oil for deep-frying in a large saucepan or wok. Dip the fish pieces, 3 at a time into the batter then straight into the hot oil and deep-fry for 3–5 minutes, making sure you rotate them, or until the batter is golden brown. Remove with a slotted spoon and drain on paper towel. Repeat with the rest of the fish, then garnish with a squeeze of lime, spring onion and chaat masala, if liked.

N O T E : To test if the oil for deep-frying is hot enough, drop in a small piece of bread, if it browns in 20 seconds it's ready.

Coriander and Chilli Crab Balls

FRAGRANT SPICE AND DELICATE CRAB ARE SUCH
AN IRRESISTIBLE COMBINATION; YOU MIGHT WANT
TO MAKE A DOUBLE QUANTITY OF THESE.

MAKES 15 BITE-SIZED BALLS | PREPARATION TIME: 50 MINUTES
COOKING TIME: 15 MINUTES

FRESH

250g smooth mashed potato

300g white crabmeat

5–6 spring onions, finely chopped

I garlic clove, very finely chopped

5mm piece ginger, peeled
and finely grated

2 red chillies, finely chopped

grated zest of 1 lime, then ½ juiced

1 tablespoon finely chopped coriander

1 egg, whisked

100g fresh breadcrumbs

SPICES

1 teaspoon ground cumin

PANTRY/LARDER

1 teaspoon salt, or to taste

3 tablespoons plain flour

oil, for deep-frying

OPTIONAL GARNISH

10cm piece daikon, finely grated and
squeezed dry with a cloth

2 tablespoons finely chopped
coriander

SERVE

1 lime, cut into wedges

1. In a large bowl, place the mashed potato, crabmeat, spring onions, garlic, ginger, chillies, lime zest and juice, 1 tablespoon chopped coriander, ground cumin and salt.

2. Using your hands, gently mix together and shape the mixture into round balls. Place each ball onto a lightly oiled plate, and refrigerate for about 15–20 minutes.

3. Meanwhile, put the whisked egg into a bowl, then spread the flour and breadcrumbs on two separate plates. Heat enough oil in a deep saucepan or wok for deep-frying.

4. Take 1 crab cake at a time and lightly coat first in the flour, then dip into the egg and finally, coat in the breadcrumbs. Deep-fry in batches of 3–4 for about 2–3 minutes, or until crisp and golden. Remove with a slotted spoon and drain on paper towel. Garnish with daikon and more coriander, if liked, and serve with lime wedges.

NOTE: To test if the oil for deep-frying is hot enough, drop in a small piece of bread, if it browns in 20 seconds it's ready.

Garlic, Ginger and Chilli Prawns

THIS CLEVER DISH IS SO SIMPLE TO PREPARE AND COOK FOR A RELAXED MEAL WITH FRIENDS. HAVE PLENTY OF CRUSTY BREAD ON HAND TO DIP INTO AND SOAK UP ALL THE SPICED BUTTER.

SERVES 4 | PREPARATION TIME: 15 MINUTES | COOKING TIME: 5 MINUTES

FRESH

200g ghee

12 raw king prawns, peeled with tails on

8 fresh curry leaves

4 garlic cloves, crushed

5cm piece ginger, peeled and sliced into thin sticks

1 large red chilli, thinly sliced

SPICES

1 teaspoon black mustard seeds

PANTRY/LARDER

1½ teaspoons oil

salt, to taste

GARNISH

2 tablespoons finely chopped coriander

3 spring onions, thinly sliced

1. Preheat the oven to 200°C/400°F/Gas 6.

2. Heat the ghee in a medium saucepan over a high heat and bring to a light boil.

3. Place four individual ramekin dishes on a baking tray.

4. Gently divide the hot ghee among the dishes and add 3 prawns to each dish.

5. Cook the prawns in the oven for 5 minutes, or until the prawns are cooked through.

6. Meanwhile, heat the oil in a small frying pan over a low–medium heat. Add the mustard seeds and curry leaves and fry for 20 seconds, then add the garlic, ginger and red chilli and fry for a further 20–30 seconds.

7. Divide the tempered spices among each prawn dish, season with salt to taste and gently stir through.

8. Finish off by garnishing with chopped coriander and sliced spring onions.

Sesame and Ginger Chicken Skewers

A SIMPLE, YET INDULGENT STARTER OR CANAPÉ, IT IS BEST SERVED
WITH CORIANDER AND PEANUT CHUTNEY (SEE PAGE 172).
TO GET AHEAD, START THIS RECIPE THE NIGHT BEFORE BY MARINATING
THE CHICKEN, OMITTING THE EGGS AND FLOUR UNTIL YOU ARE
READY TO COOK. DRIZZLE WITH HONEY AND EAT IMMEDIATELY.

SERVES 2–3 | PREPARATION TIME: 40 MINUTES
MARINATING TIME: 30 MINUTES–8 HOURS | COOKING TIME: 40 MINUTES

FRESH

2 skinless, boneless chicken breasts

1 green chilli, thinly sliced

1 garlic clove, crushed

45g piece ginger, peeled

2 tablespoons finely chopped coriander

2 tablespoons fresh lime or lemon juice

1 egg white

SPICES

¾ teaspoon garam masala

PANTRY/LARDER

40g white sesame seeds

2 tablespoons soy sauce

¼ teaspoon salt

oil, for deep-frying

3 teaspoons plain flour

OPTIONAL GARNISH

honey, to drizzle

1. Cut each chicken breast into 8–9 pieces or cubes and place in a deep bowl.

2. Gently pulse the chilli, garlic, ginger, coriander, lime juice, garam masala, sesame seeds, soy sauce and salt in a blender for 30–40 seconds.

3. Pour the mixture over the chicken pieces, and, using your hands, gently rub into the pieces until coated. Cover and chill for 30 minutes, or overnight.

4. Heat the oil for deep-frying in a deep saucepan to 180°C/350°F.

5. Mix the egg white and flour into the chicken and mix until everything is well coated. Deep-fry the chicken in 2 batches for 3–4 minutes on both sides until golden. Remove with a slotted spoon and drain on paper towel. Lightly drizzle with honey. Thread onto wooden skewers and serve immediately.

N O T E : To test if the oil for deep-frying is hot enough, drop in a small piece of bread, if it browns in 20 seconds it's ready.

HOW TO MAKE
Paneer

PANEER IS AN INDIAN CHEESE WHERE THE MILK IS COAGULATED BY ADDING A FOOD ACID. IT'S NOT A FERMENTED OR CURED PRODUCT LIKE OTHER CHEESES. THE COAGULATED MILK SHREDS ARE COLLECTED IN MUSLIN (CHEESECLOTH) AND HUNG OR PRESSED WITH A HEAVY WEIGHT. AFTER COOLING, A BLOCK OF PANEER HAS FORMED, WHICH CAN BE USED FOR MAKING A VARIETY OF DISHES. ALTHOUGH WIDELY AVAILABLE IN SUPERMARKETS, THERE IS SOMETHING SPECIAL AND UNIQUE ABOUT MAKING YOUR OWN.

MAKES ABOUT 250G | PREPARATION TIME: 1–2 HOURS | COOKING TIME: 4–5 MINUTES

EQUIPMENT

HEAVY-BASED SAUCEPAN
MUSLIN, COLANDER,
MEASURING JUG,
THERMOMETER

80°C

Strain

Stir

1

In a heavy-based saucepan, heat 1 litre full-cream (whole) milk. Bring the milk to a temperature just below boiling point, then turn off the heat. It should be about 80°C/175°F.

2

Immediately add 3–4 tablespoons of lemon juice, 1 teaspoon at a time, gently stirring the milk after each addition and making sure the mixture doesn't stick to the base of the pan. Keep stirring until the milk separates and the solid curds part from the green and watery whey. Turn off the heat.

Note You can always substitute lemon juice with lime juice or white wine vinegar.

3

Allow the curds and whey to cool for 30 minutes, or until still warm, but at a temperature you can handle. In the sink, line a deep colander with a large piece of muslin. Slowly strain the mixture through the muslin. Rinse the curds gently with fresh water.

4

Pull together the muslin corners, wrap around and tie tightly into a knot. While doing so squeeze out moisture from the curds. The more you squeeze, the firmer the resulting paneer shall be.

Note This is tricky, so be gentle and patient.

Squeeze

5

In a sink, position the wrapped paneer between two chopping boards. This way you can force out more moisture, and shape it into a firmer block, suitable for slicing and frying. To get a more rectangular shape, place something heavy like a pile of books, measuring weights or a small saucepan of water straight on top of the upper chopping board. This will create extra pressure and give the cheese its familiar box shape. The longer you press the cheese, the firmer it gets – about 30–40 minutes is ideal.

Press

Cut

6

Unwrap the paneer to find a firm block. Chop or slice the paneer into any shape or size you want. A great way to keep paneer soft is to soak the whole paneer block in a bowl of water and keep it in the refrigerator. This way the paneer does not become hard. Alternatively, you can soak the paneer in warm water after you have removed it from the refrigerator. Use it immediately or refrigerate for up to 2 days. Paneer also freezes very well.

Paneer and Pepper Filo Cigars

PANEER IS A MELLOW CHEESE THAT CARRIES SPICE VERY WELL. YOU CAN MAKE THESE VEGETARIAN BITES WELL AHEAD; WRAP THE FILLING WITH THE FILO, BRUSH WITH BUTTER AND THEN CHILL UNTIL READY TO BAKE. SWITCH THE CAPSICUMS (PEPPERS) FOR BLANCHED SPINACH OR CHARGRILLED EGGPLANT (AUBERGINE), IF LIKED.

MAKES 15 | PREPARATION TIME: 30 MINUTES | COOKING TIME: 15 MINUTES

FRESH

200g paneer (see page 42)
3 teaspoons fenugreek leaves
⅓ packet filo pastry

SPICES

1 teaspoon ground cumin
1 teaspoon ground coriander
1 teaspoon red chilli flakes
½ teaspoon dry mango powder (amchoor)

PANTRY/LARDER

25g jarred roasted red capsicum (pepper), patted dry with paper towel
salt, to taste
flour, for dusting
100g melted ghee or butter, for brushing

OPTIONAL GARNISH

1 teaspoon each of ajwain seeds, fennel seeds and onion seeds mixed together

1. Preheat the oven to 180°C/350°F/Gas 4 and line a baking tray with baking paper.

2. Place all the ingredients, except the pastry, ghee and flour into a blender and gently pulse until well combined.

3. Lay 1 sheet of the pastry on a floured work surface and brush with melted ghee or butter, then lay another sheet on top and brush that sheet with more ghee or butter. Cut the pastry lengthways into 3 strips. Repeat until all the pastry is used.

4. Spoon the filling along 1 edge of each of the pastry strips, leaving room to fold the pastry in at each end. Roll up into cigar shapes and lay, sealed edge down, on the prepared baking tray. Repeat until all the ingredients are used.

5. Brush the cigars with ghee or butter, sprinkle with the mixed seed garnish, if liked, and bake in the oven for about 15 minutes, or until golden brown.

NOTE: If using shop-bought paneer, cut into cubes, drop into boiling water and simmer for 5–7 minutes. Drain and then use.

Chana Chaat / Bhel Puri

THIS STREET-STYLE SNACK IS A REAL TALKING POINT AND IDEAL TO SERVE
WITH DRINKS. IT'S ALL ABOUT THE CONTRASTS IN FLAVOUR AND TEXTURE,
WITH SWEET, SOUR, CRUNCHY AND SOFT ALL IN ONE BITE.

SERVES 4 | PREPARATION TIME: 20 MINUTES

FRESH

1 large potato, boiled with skin on,
cooled and cut into small cubes

3 tablespoons Coriander and
Peanut Chutney (see page 172)

3 tablespoons Fresh Tomato, Date and
Tamarind Relish (see page 176)

50g pomegranate seeds, reserving
1 tablespoon to garnish

½ red onion, finely chopped

SPICES

½ teaspoon chaat masala

PANTRY/LARDER

350g cooked chickpeas

8 tablespoons sev
(gram flour crispy noodles)

8 tablespoons puffed rice

2 tablespoons roasted cashews

1 teaspoon salt, or to taste

OPTIONAL GARNISH

finely chopped coriander, spring onion,
mint and red chilli

1 tablespoon pomegranate seeds

1. In a large bowl, gently mix together all the ingredients.

2. Garnish if liked and eat immediately.

Chicken Tikka Wraps

HOMEMADE CHICKEN TIKKA, MARINATED AND BASTED WITH GHEE, IS SUCCULENT AND SMOKY AND UTTERLY DELICIOUS WRAPPED AND EATEN HOT IN FRESH NAAN BREAD. THREAD BIG CHUNKS OF CAPSICUM (PEPPER) AND ONION ONTO THE SKEWERS TO MAKE THE FILLING MORE SUBSTANTIAL. FOR AN EVEN MORE INTENSE CHARRED FLAVOUR, COOK THE CHICKEN ON A BARBECUE.

SERVES 4 | PREPARATION TIME: 20 MINUTES
MARINATING TIME: 2–8 HOURS | COOKING TIME: 20 MINUTES

FRESH

400g skinless, boneless chicken thighs

1 quantity Tikka Masala Marinade (see page 246)

1 egg white

1 lime, cut into wedges

1 large tomato, thinly sliced

½ red onion, thinly sliced

Cucumber, Carrot and Mint Chutney (see page 182)

SPICES

1 tablespoon chaat masala (optional)

PANTRY/LARDER

1 tablespoon oil

2 tablespoons ghee, for basting

Naan Bread (see page 127)

1. Chop the chicken thighs into bite-sized pieces. Place in a bowl, coat and mix well with the Tikka Masala Marinade. Cover with plastic wrap and leave to marinate in the refrigerator for 1–2 hours, or overnight.

2. Add the egg and oil to the chicken just before cooking.

3. Preheat the grill to a medium setting. Either soak wooden skewers for 30 minutes before using or use metal ones. Thread pieces of chicken, one at a time onto each skewer. Line them up on a wire rack set over a baking tray and cook under the grill for 20 minutes, turning occasionally and basting with the ghee. Cook until the juices run clear.

4. Unthread each skewer onto a tray, sprinkle with the chaat masala, if liked, and a squeeze of lime.

5. Line up pieces of chicken in the middle of each bread, place slices of tomato and onion on top and drizzle with Cucumber, Carrot and Mint Chutney. Fold in the sides, then slice the wrap in half.

ALTERNATIVE: Instead of chicken, use paneer, parboiled chunky mixed vegetables or both. Shred the chicken, let it cool and stuff into pittas for lunchboxes.

Potato and Pea Samosas

MAKING SAMOSAS FROM SCRATCH IS AN EFFORT, BUT WORTHWHILE. WHY NOT GET OTHERS TO JOIN IN, ROLLING, FILLING AND SEALING THE SAMOSAS ON YOUR OWN LITTLE PRODUCTION LINE? IF YOU WOULD RATHER NOT FRY THE SAMOSAS, WRAP IN SHORTCRUST PASTRY AND BAKE INSTEAD.

MAKES 16–20 | PREPARATION TIME: 40 MINUTES | COOKING TIME: 30 MINUTES

FRESH

55g onion, finely chopped

55g cooked peas

2 small green chillies, thinly sliced

5mm piece ginger, peeled

550g cooked potatoes, peeled and roughly mashed

3 tablespoons finely chopped coriander

1 quantity Rich Indian Pastry (see page 250)

SPICES

1 tablespoon cumin seeds

1 tablespoon coriander seeds, lightly crushed

½ teaspoon garam masala

1½ teaspoons fenugreek leaves

PANTRY/LARDER

2 tablespoons oil, plus extra for deep-frying

1½ teaspoons salt, or to taste

1 tablespoon plain flour, plus extra for dusting

1. Heat the 2 tablespoons oil in a large frying pan over a low–medium heat. Add the cumin seeds and coriander seeds and stir-fry for 20 seconds.

2. Add the onion, turn up the heat slightly and fry for 3–4 minutes until the onion is golden brown. Add the cooked peas, garam masala, chillies, ginger, fenugreek and salt and fry for 1 minute. Reduce the heat, mix in the mashed potato and chopped coriander and stir until well combined.

3. Mix together the flour and 2 tablespoons water to make a paste. Set aside.

4. Heat the oil for deep-frying in a deep saucepan to 180°C/350°F (see Note, page 52).

5. To assemble the samosas, divide the pastry dough into 4 small balls. Roll each ball into a circle about 12cm wide. Cut each circle in half. Each half moon will yield 1 samosa.

6. Add a spoonful of filling to the centre of each half-moon shape. Dip your finger in the sticky flour paste and run along the edges. Fold the side in to form a cone, making sure to seal the edges tightly. Leave on a floured tray. Work quickly to prevent the samosas drying out. Dust off any excess flour and deep-fry until golden. Remove and drain on paper towel.

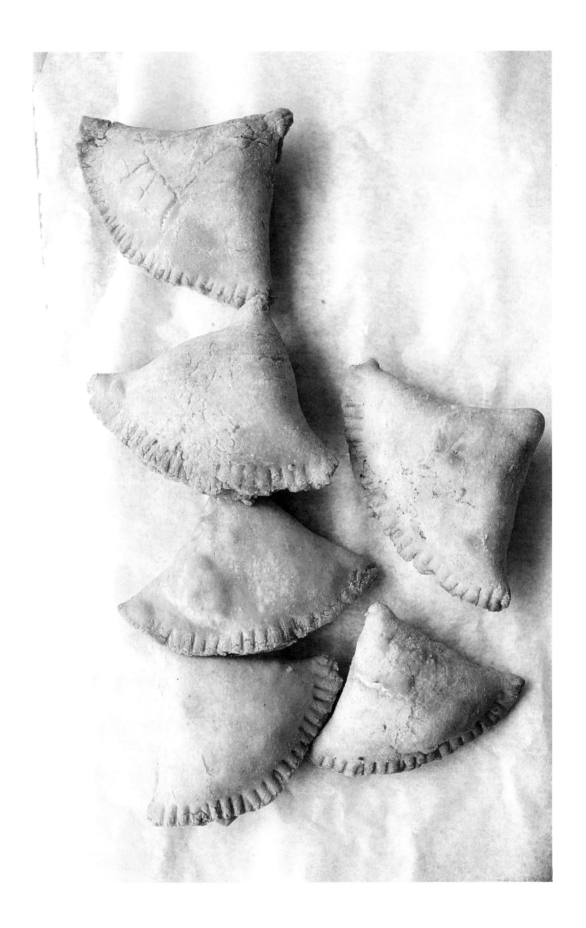

Alternative Samosa Fillings

ONCE YOU HAVE MASTERED THE BASIC RECIPE, TRY ONE OF THESE DIFFERENT FILLING IDEAS:

NOTE:

To test if the oil for deep-frying is hot enough, drop in a small piece of bread, if it browns in 20 seconds it's ready.

To prepare ahead, fry the samosas for 7–8 minutes until crisp but not yet golden, then put on a baking tray and reheat in the oven preheated to 200°C/400°F/Gas 6 until crisp and hot through.

For very crispy, flaky samosas, fry them twice – once at 180°C/350°F and the second time around at 190°C/375°F . If you plan to freeze the samosas, fry them just once. Cool completely and freeze in plastic freezer bags.

MINCED LAMB, WITH PEAS AND MINT

Follow the recipe for Lamb and Apricot Pasties (see page 32), omitting the apricots and replacing with cooked peas, and adding ½ teaspoon dried mint and ½ teaspoon chaat masala to the filling.

SHREDDED CARROT, CABBAGE AND FINELY CRUSHED ROASTED PEANUTS

1. In a bowl, mix together 120g shredded white cabbage, 2 grated carrots, 5mm piece ginger, peeled and grated, 1½ teaspoons ground cumin, 2 tablespoons roasted crushed peanuts, 1 tablespoon finely chopped coriander and salt to taste.

2. Heat 1 tablespoon oil in a frying pan over a low–medium heat, add 1 teaspoon black mustard seeds, 5–6 curry leaves and 1 thinly sliced whole red chilli and fry for 30–40 seconds, then add to the vegetables and mix together well.

SPINACH AND PANEER

1. Heat 1 tablespoon oil in a frying pan over a low–medium heat. Add 2 teaspoons cumin seeds and fry for 20 seconds. Reduce the heat to low and add 5mm piece ginger, peeled and grated, 120g paneer, cut into tiny cubes, 1½ teaspoons dried fenugreek leaves, 1 teaspoon garam masala and salt to taste, and fry for 1 minute.

2. Remove the pan from the heat and stir in 500g wilted and squeezed dry spinach. Cool completely.

SHREDDED DUCK, SPRING ONION, GINGER AND CORIANDER

In a large bowl, mix together 600g cooked shredded duck, 3 thinly sliced spring onions, 1cm piece ginger, peeled and grated, 2 teaspoons ground cumin, 1 tablespoon finely chopped coriander, 4–5 finely chopped mint leaves, 1 very finely chopped large red chilli and salt to taste.

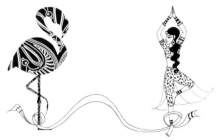

Lemon and Spice-roasted Mixed Nuts

THINK OF THESE NOT JUST AS A SNACK TO ENJOY WITH DRINKS, BUT AS AN INGREDIENT TOO. TRY CRUSHED FOR TOPPING SALADS, DIPS AND SCATTERING OVER RICE DISHES. HAZELNUTS, PISTACHIOS AND PECANS WOULD ALL WORK WELL, PLUS YOU CAN REPLACE THE SUGAR WITH A HANDFUL OF RAISINS, IF YOU LIKE.

SERVES 4 | PREPARATION TIME: 10 MINUTES | COOKING TIME: ABOUT 30 MINUTES

FRESH

grated zest and juice of 1 lemon

SPICES

1 teaspoon coarsely ground black pepper

1 teaspoon ground cumin

1 teaspoon chilli powder

½ teaspoon chaat masala

PANTRY/LARDER

2 tablespoons melted coconut oil or ghee or peanut oil

1 teaspoon soft brown sugar

1 teaspoon sea salt, or to taste

175g cashews

175g walnuts

175g almonds

175g peanuts

1. Preheat the oven to 150°C/300°F/Gas 2.

2. In a large bowl, whisk together the oil or ghee, lemon zest and juice, all the spices, sugar and salt. Next, add all the nuts and toss well, making sure all the nuts are well coated.

3. Lay out the spiced nuts evenly on a baking tray and bake in the oven for 20 minutes, making sure to toss and move the nuts around halfway. Turn down the heat to 125°C/250°F/Gas 1 and continue to bake for a further 10 minutes, or until golden brown.

4. Remove from the oven and allow to cool completely. Store in an airtight container for up to 7 days.

NOTE: Keep a close eye on them during the last 5 minutes so that the nuts don't burn.

Vegetables and Lentils

CHAPTER 2

Chana Masala

A RICH, NORTH INDIAN CHICKPEA DISH, TRADITIONALLY SERVED WITH
POORIES (PUFFED-UP FRIED BREAD), BUT ANY BREAD IS PERFECT. ANY
LEFT OVER AND THE SAUCE CAN BE DRIED OUT, DRIZZLED WITH FRESH
TOMATO, DATE AND TAMARIND RELISH (SEE PAGE 176), THEN SERVED WITH
FRIED PASTRIES OR STUFFED POTATO AND PEA CAKES (SEE PAGE 156).

SERVES 4 | PREPARATION TIME: 30 MINUTES | COOKING TIME: 15 MINUTES

FRESH
1 large onion, roughly chopped

3 garlic cloves, roughly chopped

5cm piece ginger, peeled
and roughly chopped

1½ green chillies, roughly chopped

2 tablespoons finely chopped coriander
leaves, plus extra to garnish

4 teaspoons crème fraîche

SPICES
2 teaspoons fenugreek leaves

1 teaspoon panch phoran

1 bay leaf

2.5cm piece cassia stick

1 teaspoon ground turmeric

2 teaspoons garam masala

2 teaspoons ground cumin

PANTRY/LARDER
3 tablespoons oil

760g chickpeas, reserving 2 tablespoons

2 tablespoons tomato passata
(puréed tomatoes)

1 teaspoon salt, or to taste

OPTIONAL GARNISH
1 teaspoon ghee and
¼ teaspoon chaat masala

1. Heat 1 tablespoon of the oil in a frying pan and fry the onion, garlic, ginger and green chillies for 6–7 minutes until soft and golden brown. Using a slotted spoon, place in a blender along with the 2 tablespoons chickpeas, the passata, fenugreek leaves and 180–190ml water and blitz to a smooth paste.

2. Heat the remaining oil in the same pan over a low–medium heat, add the panch phoran, bay leaf and cassia stick and fry for 30–40 seconds.

3. Pour in the chickpea paste and fry for 1 minute. Add the turmeric, garam masala, ground cumin, 1 tablespoon of the coriander and the salt and fry for a further 1 minute.

4. Mix in the remaining chickpeas and 60–70ml water, stir, then cover and simmer for 5–6 minutes. Stir in the crème fraîche and remaining coriander and cook for a further 5 minutes, or until thick and creamy.

5. Drizzle with ghee, sprinkle with chaat masala and garnish with coriander or more chaat masala and ghee.

NOTE: Combining a small amount of boiled chickpeas with caramelised onions, garlic and ginger helps create a thick, silky and smooth base. This paste can be made a day in advance.

Tarka Dhal with Spinach and Fresh Tomato

A CLASSIC, MIXED LENTIL DISH COOKED WITH WHOLE CUMIN AND GROUND SPICES, THEN GARNISHED WITH SMOKY BURNT GARLIC AND CRISPY CURRY LEAVES, GINGER AND CHILLI. EASY AND QUICK TO COOK, THIS IS PERFECT FOR FRIENDS OR FAMILY FOR SUPPER.

SERVES 4 | PREPARATION TIME: 20 MINUTES | COOKING TIME: 45 MINUTES

FRESH
¼ onion, finely chopped

2 garlic cloves, finely chopped

1cm piece ginger, peeled and finely chopped

3 large handfuls of baby spinach, chopped

1 tomato, finely diced

SPICES
½ teaspoon ground turmeric

1 teaspoon cumin seeds

1 teaspoon garam masala

PANTRY/LARDER
100g yellow mung beans

50g masoor dhal

50g toor dhal

1 teaspoon salt, or to taste

3 tablespoons oil

ghee, for drizzling

OPTIONAL GARNISH
Curry Leaves, Garlic, Ginger and Red Chilli (see page 240)

1. Wash the mung beans and both dhals together thoroughly. Put them into a large saucepan and cover with water. Bring to the boil over a high heat, then reduce the heat to medium and simmer for 15 minutes. Using a large spoon, remove any white scum or residue.

2. Add the turmeric and salt and continue to simmer for a further 10 minutes, stirring occasionally and pressing the beans and dhal against the pan with the back of your spoon. Cook until they are soft and creamy (add a little boiling water if too thick). Turn off the heat.

3. In a separate frying pan, heat the oil over a low–medium heat. Add the cumin seeds and fry for 2–3 seconds. Turn up the heat slightly, add the onion and fry for 3–4 minutes until golden brown. Add the garlic and ginger and fry for 20 seconds.

4. Add the garam masala and fry for 1 minute, then pour in a ladleful of mung beans and dhal, swirl around the pan and pour it all back into the large pan of cooked dhal. Simmer the dhal over a low heat for 8–10 minutes.

5. Turn off the heat, add the chopped spinach and tomato, drizzle with ghee and garnish with the Curry Leaves, Garlic, Ginger and Red Chilli.

Shallots with Tamarind and Toasted Coconut

THIS IS AN INTERESTING COMBINATION OF SWEET SHALLOTS, TOASTED COCONUT AND SOUR TAMARIND, INFUSED WITH CHILLIES AND CRISPY CURRY LEAVES. THIS DISH WORKS WELL AS A SIDE DISH WITH DHALS AND MOST FLAVOURED RICE AND INDIAN BREADS.

SERVES 2–3 | PREPARATION TIME: 15 MINUTES | COOKING TIME: 15 MINUTES

FRESH
150g shallots, peeled and halved lengthways
1 teaspoon tamarind pulp
7–9 fresh curry leaves

SPICES
1 teaspoon crushed coriander seeds
1 teaspoon chilli powder
¼ teaspoon ground turmeric
1 teaspoon mustard seeds
1 dried red chilli

PANTRY/LARDER
40g desiccated coconut
3 tablespoons oil
½ teaspoon salt, or to taste

1. Heat a small frying pan over a low–medium heat and dry-roast the coconut and coriander seeds until golden brown. Add the chilli powder, then turn off the heat and place in a blender. Blitz together, adding enough water, about 3–4 tablespoons, to make a smooth paste.

2. Next, heat a separate frying pan over a medium heat and pour in 2 tablespoons of the oil. Add the shallots and keep tossing and cooking until they are slightly browned. Add the salt, 3–4 tablespoons water and the turmeric and cook for 5–7 minutes, or until soft. Add the coconut paste and tamarind pulp. Reduce the heat slightly and cook for 3–5 minutes.

3. Heat a large frying pan over a low–medium heat. Pour in the remaining oil, add the mustard seeds and toss and fry for 20 seconds. Add the curry leaves and dried red chilli and fry for 15 seconds. Finally, add the cooked shallots, gently toss everything together, then serve.

Creamy Peas and Mushrooms

A RICH AND SATISFYING DISH, IT IS PRETTY QUICK TO MAKE AND DOESN'T REQUIRE OR NEED ANY ONIONS OR CHILLIES. IT IS WONDERFUL AS PART OF ANY FAMILY MEAL OR A SIMPLE BRUNCH DISH – JUST SERVE ON THICK SLICES OF TOASTED BREAD. FRY THE MUSHROOMS AND PEAS WITH SPICES IN ADVANCE, THEN WHEN READY TO SERVE, STIR IN THE CREAM, STOCK AND GENTLY SIMMER.

SERVES 4 AS A SIDE | PREPARATION TIME: 20 MINUTES | COOKING TIME: 15 MINUTES

FRESH
3 tablespoons light (single) cream

8–9 fresh curry leaves

3 garlic cloves, very finely chopped

200–250g chestnut mushrooms, cut into quarters

115g cooked peas

1cm piece ginger, peeled and cut into julienne

SPICES
large pinch of freshly grated nutmeg

1 teaspoon black mustard seeds

¼ teaspoon ground turmeric

¼ teaspoon paprika

1 teaspoon cracked black pepper

½ teaspoon garam masala

PANTRY/LARDER
2 tablespoons oil

1 tablespoon coconut milk powder

1 teaspoon salt, or to taste

100ml vegetable or chicken stock or water

OPTIONAL GARNISH
finely chopped coriander, spring onion, and green or red chilli

1. Mix together the single cream, coconut milk powder and nutmeg and set aside for later.

2. Heat the oil in a heavy-based frying pan over a low–medium heat. Add the mustard seeds and curry leaves and once they start to crackle and pop, add the garlic and mushrooms. Turn up the heat slightly and fry, stirring frequently for 5 minutes, or until the mushrooms are a rich nutty brown.

3. Next, add the peas, turmeric, paprika, pepper, garam masala and salt, and cook, stirring, for 1 minute.

4. Now pour in the reserved cream paste and the stock or water. Turn down the heat and gently simmer for 4–5 minutes. Stir in the ginger and serve garnished with coriander, spring onion and chilli.

Baigan Bharta

TO ADD A FURTHER INTENSE SMOKY FLAVOUR, COOK EGGPLANT
OVER AN OPEN FIRE OR BARBECUE. THIS CAN BE DONE A DAY IN ADVANCE.
ANY GOING SPARE CAN BE MIXED WITH NATURAL YOGHURT AND
SERVED AT ROOM TEMPERATURE.

SERVES 4 | PREPARATION TIME: 20–30 MINUTES | COOKING TIME: 30 MINUTES

FRESH

2 large eggplant (aubergines)

3 onions, finely chopped

2–3 garlic cloves, finely chopped

1cm piece ginger, peeled
and finely shredded

SPICES

1 teaspoon panch phoran (optional)

½ teaspoon ground cumin

1 bay leaf

2.5cm piece cassia or cinnamon stick

1 teaspoon fenugreek leaves

¼ teaspoon ground turmeric

1 teaspoon garam masala

½ teaspoon ground coriander

PANTRY/LARDER

4 tablespoons oil

1 teaspoon salt, or to taste

OPTIONAL GARNISH

8 cherry tomatoes, halved or quartered
and seeded if possible

1 tablespoon finely chopped coriander

FOR THOUGHT

If you have any leftovers, stir in 2 tablespoons
Greek-style yoghurt, 1 teaspoon finely
chopped mint and salt if needed, then serve
at room temperature as a cold side dish

1. Preheat the grill to a medium–high setting. Rub or brush ½ teaspoon of the oil all over the eggplant, then using a fork, pierce a few random holes all over – this helps with the removal of the skin once cooled. Place under the grill and cook, turning frequently for about 15 minutes, or until black, smoky and charred and the flesh is buttery soft. Cool, then gently peel (discard) and shred the flesh with a knife and fork and set aside.

2. Meanwhile, heat the remaining oil in a large heavy-based frying pan over a low–medium heat. Temper the following spices gently for 40 seconds: panch phoran, if using, followed by the cumin, bay leaf and cassia or cinnamon stick.

3. Next, add the onions and fry gently for 4–5 minutes, or until soft and caramelised. Turn up the heat slightly, add the garlic and fenugreek leaves, and continue to fry for 1 minute. Stir in the turmeric, garam masala, ground coriander, ginger and salt and fry for 1 minute, then add the smoky, cooked eggplant, mix well and continue cooking, stirring frequently to avoid sticking, for 5–7 minutes. Cover with a lid and cook for a further 4 minutes. Serve garnished with tomatoes and coriander, if liked.

Cauliflower and Peas

THERE ARE SEVERAL WAYS OF MAKING THIS DISH, BUT THIS ONE
IS AN EASY-GOING AND SIMPLIFIED VERSION. CONSIDER
OTHER VEGETABLES SUCH AS BUTTERNUT PUMPKIN,
BROCCOLI OR EVEN PANEER. IF SHORT ON TIME, PARBOIL
THE CAULIFLOWER AND REDUCE THE COOKING TIME.

SERVES 4 | PREPARATION TIME: 15 MINUTES | COOKING TIME: 15 MINUTES

FRESH

850g cauliflower, cut into
bite-sized pieces

1 green chilli, slit lengthways
down the middle

200g cooked peas

SPICES

1¼ teaspoons ground turmeric

2 teaspoons crushed coriander seeds

2 teaspoons crushed fennel seeds

1 teaspoon ground cumin

PANTRY/LARDER

1 teaspoon plain flour

½ teaspoon salt, or to taste

2 tablespoons mustard seed oil
(see page 15) or oil

90 ml tomato passata
(puréed tomatoes)

OPTIONAL GARNISH

crispy curry leaves, garlic, ginger
and red or green chilli

1. Place the cauliflower in a large bowl, sprinkle with the flour, turmeric, salt and 1 tablespoon of the oil and rub into the florets until they are well coated.

2. Heat the remaining mustard oil in a large frying pan or a wok over a medium heat. Add the cauliflower and green chilli and keep tossing and frying for 5–6 minutes until half-cooked and a little charred.

3. Add the crushed coriander and fennel seeds and ground cumin and fry for 1 minute.

4. Reduce the heat slightly, add the passata and cooked peas, then cover with a lid and continue to fry, stirring frequently for 6–7 minutes until cooked through.

5. Garnish with crispy curry leaves, garlic, ginger and red or green chilli, if liked.

SIX

Eggs

❶ MASALA SCRAMBLED EGGS

WHISK 8 eggs in a bowl, add 2 tablespoons light (single) cream or milk and whisk together.

HEAT 1 tablespoon oil in a heavy-based frying pan over a low heat.

ADD ½ teaspoon cumin seeds and 2.5cm piece ginger, peeled and shredded, and fry gently for 10 seconds.

ADD ½–1 teaspoon garam masala, 1 teaspoon red chilli flakes and a little salt and fry for 1 minute.

POUR in the eggs and reduce the heat. Stir gently from side to side until you get near enough to a rich creamy consistency.

DRIZZLE with 2 teaspoons ghee, and finely chopped coriander.

SERVE with plain paranthas (see note,page 120) or toasted muffins.

❷ SPICED EGGY BREAD

WHISK 6 eggs into a large wide, flat bowl.

ADD 1 teaspoon garam masala, ½ teaspoon ground cumin, ½ teaspoon ground coriander, 1 tablespoon fenugreek leaves, 1 teaspoon red chilli flakes, 2 tablespoons finely chopped coriander and ½ teaspoon salt. Whisk everything together.

PLACE a heavy-based frying pan over a medium heat.

ADD 2 tablespoons oil and a large knob of butter. Take 4–5 thin slices of bread, dip 1 slice of bread at a time into the egg mixture pressing gently, then flip over until well coated and leave to soak for a minute or two.

PLACE your bread slice into the hot pan and fry until golden and crisp on both sides.

SERVE immediately.

❸ COCONUT EGG CURRY

HEAT the oil in a wok or heavy-based frying pan and gently fry 6 soft–medium boiled eggs for 1 minute until lightly golden. Remove and reserve.

ADD 1 tablespoon Ginger and Garlic Paste (see page 231), 1 tablespoon Caramelised Onion Paste (see page 231), followed by 1½ teaspoons ground turmeric, 1½ teaspoons garam masala, 1 teaspoon ground cumin and ½ teaspoon salt.

FRY for 30–35 seconds while gently tossing.

STIR in 150ml coconut milk and simmer very gently over a medium heat for 2–3 minutes.

ADD 2 sliced green chillies and 6cm piece ginger, peeled and shredded, and simmer for 5 minutes, or until the sauce has thickened. Halve the eggs and add to the sauce, yolk side up. Sprinkle with finely chopped spring onion and coriander.

SERVE with Lemon and Chickpea Rice (page 146).

❹ NARGISI EGG KOFTA

BLEND 1 small onion, finely chopped (squeezed dry in a cloth), 1 tablespoon chopped ginger, 5 finely chopped garlic cloves, a pinch of nutmeg, ½ teaspoon garam masala, ½ teaspoon ground cumin, ½ teaspoon ground coriander, 1 teaspoon salt, ½ teaspoon chopped mint and 1 tablespoon chopped coriander.

BLITZ until finely chopped, then add 500g lamb mince and blitz again until it is a smooth paste.

DIVIDE the paste into 4 portions. Flatten and shape around 4 small soft-medium boiled eggs.

TAKE each kofta and roll in 4 tablespoons plain flour, then 1 beaten egg, and lastly, fresh breadcrumbs (3 slices of bread, crusts off). Chill for 30 minutes.

HEAT 1.5 litres oil over a low–medium heat and fry 2 koftas at a time for 8–10 minutes. Cut in half.

SERVE with Fresh Tomato, Date and Tamarind Relish (see page 176).

❺ ROAST VEGETABLES AND BAKED EGGS

PREHEAT the oven to 190°C/375°F/Gas 5.

COAT 250g cubed eggplant, 1 cubed yellow capsicum (pepper) and 1 chopped red onion with 25ml oil, 1 teaspoon salt, 1 teaspoon crushed fennel seeds and ½ teaspoon crushed dried red chillies.

PLACE all the vegetables on a heavy-based baking tray and roast for 15–20 minutes, tossing frequently.

MIX together with the Tomato and Mustard Dressing (see page 74) and pour everything into a shallow ovenproof dish.

MAKE 4–5 evenly spaced wells and crack 4–5 eggs, one by one into each well. Season with salt and pepper and bake for about 10–12 minutes.

GARNISH with finely chopped coriander and a pinch of toasted crushed cumin seeds.

SERVE with warm crusty bread.

❻ SPINACH AND POTATO OMELETTE

HEAT 2 tablespoons oil in a non-stick ovenproof frying pan that is about 25cm in diameter.

TOSS in 2 teaspoons whole cumin seeds, then stir in 500g cooked cubed potatoes and 3 thinly sliced spring onions and fry for 2 minutes.

CRACK 6 eggs into a large bowl, whisk and season with ½ teaspoon salt and ½ teaspoon pepper, then mix in 225g cooked chopped spinach, 1 teaspoon fenugreek leaves and ½ teaspoon red chilli flakes.

POUR the egg mixture into the frying pan. Cover and cook, without stirring, for about 6 minutes, or until the omelette is cooked but soft on top.

FINISH cooking under a very hot grill until golden brown. Cut into quarters.

SERVE with Shredded Raw Veg Salad (page 160).

Dhal Makhani

MAKE THIS MIXED LENTIL AND BEAN COMBINATION ON SPECIAL OCCASIONS, AS IT IS THE ULTIMATE STATEMENT DHAL DISH. TRADITIONALLY IT TAKES HOURS TO COOK, BUT GOOD-QUALITY, COOKED PULSES WORK JUST AS WELL. THE SMOKY GARLIC MIXED WITH THE METHI LEAVES AND CHILLIES COMBINED WITH CREAM AND BUTTER CERTAINLY MAKES THIS DISH HEAVENLY, LAVISH AND INDULGENT.

SERVES 4 | PREPARATION TIME: 30 MINUTES | COOKING TIME: 25–30 MINUTES

FRESH
1 large onion, roughly chopped
4 garlic cloves, roughly chopped
2.5cm piece ginger, peeled and roughly chopped
1 small green chilli, roughly chopped
1 tablespoon finely chopped coriander

SPICES
1½ teaspoons dried fenugreek leaves
1 teaspoon cumin seeds
2.5cm piece cassia or cinnamon stick
1 bay leaf
1 black cardamom pod, slightly crushed
¼ teaspoon ground turmeric
1½ teaspoons garam masala

PANTRY/LARDER
3 tablespoons ghee or oil
100g cooked whole black urad, reserving 1½ teaspoons
100g cooked kidney beans, reserving 1½ teaspoons
2 teaspoons tomato passata (puréed tomatoes)
1 teaspoon salt, or to taste

GARNISH
1 teaspoon ghee
1½ teaspoons double cream
1 tablespoon chopped coriander

1. Heat 1 tablespoon of the ghee or oil in a large frying pan over a low–medium heat and fry the onion, garlic, ginger and green chilli for 7–8 minutes until soft and golden brown. Cool slightly, then with a slotted spoon place in a blender together with the reserved urad and kidney beans, the tomato passata, fenugreek leaves and 50ml water and blitz to a smooth paste.

2. Heat the remaining oil in a frying pan over a low–medium heat. Add the cumin seeds, cassia or cinnamon stick, bay leaf and black cardamom and fry for 20 seconds. Add the onion and bean paste and stir-fry for 2 minutes.

3. Add the turmeric, garam masala and salt and fry for 1 minute.

4. Next, add the kidney beans, black urad, coriander and 100–120ml water, then cover with a lid and continue simmering for 10 minutes, or until thick and creamy.

5. Turn off the heat and drizzle with the ghee and cream and garnish with chopped coriander.

NOTE: Combining a small amount of boiled kidney beans with caramelised onions, garlic and ginger helps to create a thick, silky and smooth base. This paste can be made a day in advance.

Steamed Green Beans in Tomato and Mustard Dressing

THESE BEANS COMPLEMENT MOST ROASTS OR BARBECUED MEATS, SALADS AND SAVOURY TARTS. THIS SIDE DISH HAS A DELICIOUS DRESSING, WHICH CAN ALSO BE USED WITH COOKED POTATOES, PEAS, BROAD BEANS OR BROCCOLI. PREPARE THE DRESSING 1–2 DAYS IN ADVANCE, THEN WHEN DRESSING THE BEANS MAKE SURE THEY ARE HOT – THAT WAY THEY WILL ABSORB ALL THE FLAVOURS.

SERVES 4 | PREPARATION TIME: 15 MINUTES | COOKING TIME: 15 MINUTES

FRESH

250g green beans, topped and tailed

6–7 fresh curry leaves

1 garlic clove, very finely chopped

SPICES

¼ teaspoon black mustard seeds

¼ teaspoon ground turmeric

¼ teaspoon ground cinnamon

¼ teaspoon ground black pepper

¼ teaspoon ground coriander

¼ teaspoon chilli powder

PANTRY/LARDER

2 tablespoons mustard seed or vegetable oil

large pinch of sugar

180ml tomato passata (puréed tomatoes)

salt, to taste

GARNISH

Crispy Ginger, Onion and Garlic (see page 238)

1. Steam the green beans for 4–5 minutes, then drain and plunge into ice-cold water.

2. Pour the oil into a heavy-based frying pan and heat over a medium heat for 1 minute. (If using mustard oil see page 15.) Add the curry leaves and black mustard seeds and fry for 30 seconds. Turn down the heat, add the garlic and fry for 2 seconds, then add the turmeric, cinnamon, black pepper, coriander, chilli powder and sugar and fry for a further 1 minute.

3. Stir in the passata and salt to taste, and cover with a lid. Turn up the heat slightly and cook for a further 5–8 minutes, stirring occasionally, until the oil starts to separate from the tomato dressing.

4. Pour the dressing over the green beans, garnish with the Crispy Ginger, Onion and Garlic and serve hot or cold.

Beetroot Curry

DELICIOUS HOT OR COLD, BEETROOT CURRY IS A FANTASTIC MAIN COURSE
OR ACCOMPANIMENT. WHETHER YOU ARE A VEGETARIAN OR NOT, THIS
COLOURFUL MOUTH-WATERING DISH IS A HEALTHY OPTION THAT CAN
BE ENJOYED WITH A SALAD OR WITH RICE AND CHAPATI. REMEMBER TO
ENSURE THAT THE BEETROOT CHUNKS ARE ROUGHLY EQUAL IN SIZE.

SERVES 4 | PREPARATION TIME: 30 MINUTES | COOKING TIME: 40 MINUTES

FRESH

2 green chillies, slit lengthways
down the middle

2.5cm piece ginger, peeled
and roughly chopped

400–500g red beetroot

10 fresh curry leaves

1 onion, finely chopped

SPICES

4 black cardamom pods, seeds only

½ teaspoon fennel seeds

2 teaspoons black mustard seeds

½ teaspoon chilli powder

1 teaspoon ground cumin

1 teaspoon ground turmeric

PANTRY/LARDER

30g desiccated coconut

2–3 tablespoons oil

1 teaspoon salt, or to taste

SERVE

225g natural yoghurt

1. In a mixer or grinder, place the coconut, chillies, ginger, black cardamom seeds and fennel seeds and grind firmly, adding a little water if sticking. Set aside.

2. Cut the beetroot into wedges or cubes and cook in a saucepan of boiling water for 20 minutes, or until tender, then drain and set aside.

3. Heat the oil in a large frying pan. Add the mustard seeds and as they begin to pop, add the curry leaves. Immediately stir in the beetroot, onion, chilli powder, cumin, turmeric and salt and cook for 7–8 minutes, stirring frequently. Stir in the coconut spice mix, then reduce the heat and cook for a further 5 minutes over a medium heat, stirring frequently and gradually adding water to loosen, then cook for a further 5–7 minutes.

4. Remove the pan from the heat and serve with the yoghurt on top.

Kidney Beans and Potato

THE ULTIMATE IN COMFORT FOOD, AND A WARMING WINTER DISH, THIS
RUSTIC DISH HAS A DENSE MASALA BASE SAUCE, WHICH IS BEST SERVED
AND SOAKED UP WITH SIMPLE PLAIN RICE (SEE PAGE 134).

SERVES 4 | PREPARATION TIME: 20 MINUTES | COOKING TIME: 25 MINUTES

FRESH

2 onions, roughly chopped

4 garlic cloves, roughly chopped

2.5cm piece ginger, peeled
and roughly chopped

1½ green chillies, roughly chopped

1 potato, cubed into 8 pieces

2 tablespoons finely chopped coriander,
plus extra to garnish

SPICES

2 teaspoons fenugreek leaves

1½ teaspoons cumin seeds

1 teaspoon ground turmeric

1 teaspoon ground coriander

2 teaspoons garam masala

PANTRY/LARDER

3 tablespoons oil

760g cooked kidney beans,
reserving 2 tablespoons

1 tablespoon passata

1 teaspoon salt, or to taste

1 tablespoon melted ghee

1. Heat 1 tablespoon of the oil in a frying pan over a medium heat and fry the onions, garlic, ginger and green chillies for 6–7 minutes until soft and golden brown. Cool slightly, then using a slotted spoon, place in a blender together with 1 tablespoon of the reserved kidney beans, the passata, fenugreek leaves and 2 tablespoons hot water and blitz to a smooth paste.

2. Heat the remaining oil in a frying pan over a low–medium heat, add the cumin seeds and fry for 2–3 seconds. Add the onion and bean paste and fry for 2 minutes. Add the turmeric, ground coriander, garam masala and salt and fry for 1 minute, then add the potatoes and 120–140ml hot water. Cover and simmer for 5 minutes. Next, add the kidney beans and chopped coriander and continue simmering for 4–5 minutes, or until thick, creamy and the potatoes are cooked through.

3. Drizzle with the ghee and garnish with chopped coriander.

N O T E : Combining a small amount of boiled kidney beans with caramelised onions, garlic and ginger helps to create a thick, silky and smooth base. This paste can be made a day in advance.

Stuffed Okra

IT'S THE CRISP AND FRESH TEXTURE THAT MAKES OKRA THE PERFECT VEGETABLE FOR THIS DISH. ONCE YOU GET RID OF OKRA'S NATURAL 'SLIMY NATURE' BY TRIMMING THE TOPS AND ADDING LEMON JUICE, THE INCREDIBLE FLAVOURS OF THE STUFFING OOZE OUT AND COMPLEMENT THE NATURAL TASTE OF THIS 'LADIES FINGER' (AS IT IS SOMETIMES REFERRED TO IN INDIA). STUFFED OKRA IS EQUALLY GOOD AS A SIDE DISH OR A MAIN COURSE. MAKE SURE THEY ARE SUPER-DRY BEFORE PREPARING.

SERVES 4 | PREPARATION TIME: 45 MINUTES | COOKING TIME: 20 MINUTES

FRESH
500g okra
2 teaspoons lemon juice
1 red onion, thinly sliced
1 red capsicum (pepper), cut into strips
2.5cm piece ginger, peeled and thinly sliced

SPICES
1 teaspoon red chilli flakes
2 teaspoons ground coriander
2 teaspoons ground cumin
½ teaspoon dried pomegranate seed powder (optional)
1 teaspoon ground turmeric

PANTRY/LARDER
1 tablespoon desiccated coconut
1 teaspoon salt, or to taste
2–3 tablespoons oil

1. Wash and then wipe the okra until absolutely dry. Carefully remove the stalks (making sure not to cut too far down), then cut down the middle of each one from top to tail without cutting them all the way through.

2. Mix the red chilli flakes, ground coriander, ground cumin, pomegranate seed powder, if using, turmeric, desiccated coconut, the lemon juice and ¼ teaspoon of the salt, or to taste, into a paste. Using a small teaspoon, stuff each okra with this masala paste, and push in gently with your finger. Keep the leftover masala separately.

3. Heat the oil in a wok or large frying pan over a medium heat. Add the sliced onion and cook for 30 seconds, then add the stuffed okra and fry for 5 minutes tossing gently.

4. Cover with a lid and cook over a low heat, stirring occasionally. Add the red capsicum, sliced ginger and the remaining salt, turn up the heat to medium and stir-fry gently for 5–7 minutes. Cover again and cook for a further 5–6 minutes.

5. Stir in the leftover masala paste when the okra is almost cooked. Cover and cook over a low heat for 1–2 minutes, or until the okra is fully tender and darker in colour.

Wilted Spinach with Ginger, Garlic and Almonds

THIS IS A HUMBLE YET SURPRISING DISH THAT CAN BE MADE IN MINUTES. CHOOSE GOOD-QUALITY FRESH SPINACH OR EVEN CONSIDER USING SHREDDED KALE. THE LAVISH GARNISH TAKES THIS DISH TO ANOTHER LEVEL.

SERVES 2–4 AS A SIDE | PREPARATION TIME: 20 MINUTES | COOKING TIME: 3 MINUTES

FRESH

1 large red chilli, thinly sliced

1 tablespoon finely chopped onion

550g wilted or cooked fresh spinach, squeezed dry of all water and roughly chopped

2 tablespoons light (single) cream

SPICES

¼ teaspoon ground turmeric

¼ teaspoon ground cumin

PANTRY/LARDER

1 tablespoon oil

salt, to taste

GARNISH

Crispy Ginger, Onion and Garlic (see page 238)

1 tablespoon lightly toasted flaked almonds

1 teaspoon ghee

1. Heat the oil in a frying pan over a low–medium heat, then add the onion and fry for 2 minutes until golden brown.

2. Reduce the heat, add the turmeric and fry for about 30 seconds. Stir in the red chilli, cumin and salt to taste, then sir in the spinach and cream and gently heat over a low heat for 30 seconds.

3. Garnish with the Crispy Ginger, Onion and Garlic, toasted flaked almonds and a drizzle of ghee.

Charred Broccoli with Chilli and Fennel

YOU MAY THINK THAT THIS DISH IS RELAXED, BUT DON'T BE DECEIVED –
THE CHARRED BROCCOLI AND INTENSE COMBINATION OF
FENNEL, CRISPY GINGER AND GARLIC MAKE AN IMPRESSIVE STATEMENT.
OTHER VEGETABLES TO CONSIDER USING ARE ZUCCHINI (COURGETTE)
WEDGES, SLICED SWEET POTATOES OR EGGPLANT (AUBERGINE) BATONS.

SERVES 4 | PREPARATION TIME: 10 MINUTES | COOKING TIME: 6 MINUTES

FRESH

2 garlic cloves, thinly sliced

1 large red chilli, seeded (optional)
and thinly sliced

600g broccoli spears,
cut down the middle

2.5cm piece ginger, peeled
and cut into julienne

SPICES

1 teaspoon mustard seeds

2 teaspoons fennel seeds

PANTRY/LARDER

1½ tablespoons oil

salt, to taste

GARNISH

Toasted Coconut, Pomegranate Seed
and Coriander (see page 238)
handful of coriander leaves and stalks

1. Heat the oil in a large deep frying pan over a low–medium heat. Add the mustard seeds and fennel seeds and fry until they crackle and pop.

2. Add the garlic, chilli and broccoli and fry until the broccoli is slightly charred in colour. Reduce the heat, cover and cook for 4–5 minutes, until cooked through.
NOTE: You can also blanch the broccoli spears for 1–2 minutes in boiling salted water then drain.

3. Uncover, season with salt to taste and add the ginger. Toss through and gently cook for 20 seconds.

4. Garnish with a scattering of Toasted Coconut, Pomegranate Seed and Coriander and more coriander leaves and stalks.

Eggplant with Chilli and Pomegranate Dressing

THIS IS AN UPDATED VERSION OF 'TAWA BAINGAN'. COOK THE EGGPLANT SLICES UNTIL CRISP AND GOLDEN, THEN COAT AND LEAVE TO INFUSE IN THE SWEET-CHILLI DRESSING. ENJOY AS A WARM SALAD OR SIDE DISH SERVED ALONGSIDE ANY HOT CURRIES, FRIED PASTRIES AND SPICED MEATS OR BAKED FISH. ALTERNATIVELY, THE DRESSING CAN BE SERVED ON THE SIDE.

SERVES 2 AS A MAIN OR 4 AS A SIDE | PREPARATION TIME: 1 HOUR
COOKING TIME: 45 MINUTES

FRESH

2–3 small–medium eggplant (aubergines), cut into medium slices lengthways (top to tail) or small ones cut in half and scored

2 shallots, finely chopped

1 garlic clove, very finely chopped

1 tablespoon finely chopped coriander

1 tablespoon finely chopped mint

2–3 tablespoons pomegranate seeds

SPICES

¼ teaspoon ground turmeric

1 tablespoon garam masala

1 teaspoon red chilli flakes

PANTRY/LARDER

3–4 teaspoons salt, or to taste

2 tablespoons oil, plus extra for brushing

1 tablespoon sugar

3 tablespoons sherry vinegar

1. Sprinkle the eggplant slices with salt, place in a colander set over a bowl and leave to stand for 30 minutes. Rinse the eggplant and pat dry.

2. Place the turmeric and garam masala in a small bowl, together with the oil and stir together to make a paste.

3. In a small saucepan over a medium heat, combine the shallots, garlic, sugar, vinegar, red chilli flakes and 3 tablespoons water. Bring to the boil and cook for 1 minute, then remove from the heat and cool completely. Stir in the coriander, mint and pomegranate seeds.

4. Rub both sides of the eggplant slices with the mixed spice paste.

5. Heat a chargrill pan to high and brush the grates or bars with vegetable oil, then cook the eggplant until charred and tender, turning over halfway through, about 8–9 minutes.

6. Arrange the eggplant slices on a platter and spoon the dressing mixture over the over top.

NOTE: Salting the eggplant removes some of its water, which makes for better searing.

Fresh Tomato and Curry Leaf

ALTHOUGH, THIS IS A SIMPLE TOMATO DISH, IT MAKES A PERFECT SIDE DISH PARTNER FOR MOST MAIN MEAT, VEGETABLE AND RICE DISHES. HOWEVER, IT CAN ALSO BE A STAND-ALONE DISH. ENJOY WITH HOT BUTTERED NAAN (SEE PAGE 127) OR TOASTED CRUSTY BREAD.

SERVES 2–4 | PREPARATION TIME: 15 MINUTES | COOKING TIME: 15 MINUTES

FRESH

8 tomatoes, peeled, quartered and seeded

1 onion, finely chopped

3 garlic cloves, roughly chopped

8–9 fresh curry leaves

SPICES

5 whole dried chillies, soaked in 3–4 tablespoons hot water for 5 minutes

¼ teaspoon ground turmeric

1 teaspoon ground cinnamon

1½ teaspoons garam masala

large pinch freshly grated nutmeg

1 teaspoon mustard seeds

PANTRY/LARDER

2 tablespoons tomato paste (concentrated purée)

¼ teaspoon sugar

2 teaspoons coconut milk powder (optional)

2 tablespoons mustard seed oil or vegetable oil

salt, to taste

OPTIONAL GARNISH

Crispy Okra (see page 232)

1 tablespoon finely chopped coriander

1. Place the following into a blender and blitz to form a fine, smooth paste: 2 tablespoons of the tomatoes, the onion, garlic, soaked chillies (including the soaking water), tomato paste, turmeric, sugar, ground cinnamon, garam masala, nutmeg, coconut milk powder and 25ml hot water.

2. Heat the oil in a large frying pan over a low–medium heat. Add the mustard seeds and curry leaves and fry for 20 seconds.

3. Turn down the heat and stir in the tomato and coconut paste, and salt to taste. Keep stirring and frying for 1–2 minutes.

4. Pour in 25–35ml hot water, cover and simmer gently for 10 minutes, then add the remaining tomatoes, stir through and cook for 1 minute. Turn off the heat and garnish with Crispy Okra and coriander.

Fish, Meat and Poultry

CHAPTER 3

Squid with Shallots, Ginger and Chilli

A SEAFOOD LOVER'S ESSENTIAL, THE SPICED SQUID BURSTS WITH THE
SUBTLE YET UNMISTAKABLE TASTE OF THE INDIAN TRINITY OF SHALLOTS,
GINGER AND RED CHILLI, TRANSPORTING YOU TO THE BEACHES OF
KERALA, WHERE INDIAN CIVILISATION BEGAN. AN IMPRESSIVE DISH,
SERVE AS A STARTER, LIGHT LUNCH OR AT A DINNER PARTY.

SERVES 4 | PREPARATION TIME: 20 MINUTES | COOKING TIME: 15 MINUTES

FRESH

1kg fresh squid, dried well, scored and
cut into thick strips, tentacles included

8–10 fresh curry leaves

3 shallots or 1 onion,
thinly sliced

65g piece ginger, peeled
and finely shredded

1 large red chilli, seeded (optional)
and thinly sliced

2 tomatoes, finely chopped

juice of ½ lime or lemon

1 tablespoon finely chopped coriander

SPICES

1 teaspoon chilli powder

1 teaspoon ground cumin

1 teaspoon ground coriander

½ teaspoon ground turmeric

PANTRY/LARDER

85g plain flour or 42g cornflour

½ teaspoon salt, or to taste

large pinch of cracked black pepper

150ml oil

1. In a large bowl, place the flour, salt, black pepper and all
the spices. Mix well and add the squid pieces. Using clean
dry hands, toss the squid gently in the flour mix, making
sure each piece is evenly coated.

2. Heat 3 tablespoons of the oil in a large frying pan or wok
over a low–medium heat. Add the curry leaves, followed
by the shallots and fry for 2–3 minutes. Turn the heat up to
medium, add the ginger and red chilli and stir-fry until crisp
and golden brown. Remove from the pan with a slotted
spoon and drain on paper towel.

3. Using the same pan or wok, heat the remaining oil over
a low–medium heat. Add the squid in 2 batches and fry for
about 3–5 minutes until crisp and cooked through. Remove
the squid with a slotted spoon to drain.

4. Mix the squid together with the crispy shallot mix. Add
the tomatoes and toss together gently. Finish off with a
squeeze of lime or lemon and the coriander.

NOTE: Be careful not to overcook the squid.

Masala Roast Lamb

COOKING MEAT ON THE BONE DEFINITELY ADDS MORE FLAVOUR JUST
LIKE IN THIS CLASSIC RECIPE, WHICH IS A PERFECT TWIST TO A
TRADITIONAL FAMILY ROAST DINNER. ALTERNATIVELY, ENJOY THIS DISH
WITH BUTTERED STEAMED VEGETABLES AND GREEN SALAD OR THINLY
SLICED AND WRAPPED INSIDE NAAN BREAD (SEE PAGE 127).

SERVES 4–6 | PREPARATION TIME: 1 ½ HOURS
MARINATING TIME: 2–8 HOURS | COOKING TIME: 4 HOURS

FRESH

2–2.5kg leg of lamb or shoulder

500g (4–5) onions,
finely chopped

3–4 green chillies

10 garlic cloves, finely chopped

4cm piece ginger, peeled
and finely grated

500g Greek-style yoghurt,
lightly whisked

SPICES

2 tablespoons ground cumin

3 tablespoons ground coriander

1 teaspoon garam masala

4 bay leaves

2 x 2.5cm pieces cassia
or cinnamon sticks

13 green cardamom pods,
slightly cracked

12 black peppercorns

8 cloves

PANTRY/LARDER

50g ground almonds

2 teaspoons salt, or to taste

4 tablespoons oil

OPTIONAL GARNISH

1 lemon, cut into wedges

1. Using a sharp knife, make deep insertions all over the lamb, then place it in the centre of a well greased roasting tray.

2. Blitz the onions, almonds, green chillies, garlic and ginger in a blender to a paste, adding a little water if necessary to make it smooth.

3. In a bowl, mix together the yoghurt, ground cumin, ground coriander, garam masala and salt, then add the onion paste and mix well.

4. Pour the marinade over the lamb and, using your hands, massage all over, making sure to push the marinade into the insertions and that the lamb is well covered. Cover with plastic wrap and refrigerate for 2–3 hours, or overnight.

5. Remove the lamb from the refrigerator and allow to come up to room temperature. Preheat the oven to 220°C/425°F/Gas 7.

6. Heat the oil in a frying pan over a medium heat. Add the bay leaves, cassia or cinnamon, cardamom, peppercorns and cloves and fry for 30 seconds, or until slightly changed in colour.

7. Pour the whole spices over the marinated meat, add a splash of water and cover tightly with foil.

8. Place the lamb in the hot oven. Cook the lamb for up to 3–4 hours, or until the meat falls away from the bone. Reduce the heat to 130°C/250°F/Gas 1 after the first 30 minutes and uncover after the first 2 hours.

9. Allow to rest for 15–20 minutes. Garnish with lemon wedges, if liked.

Mussels in Chilli, Ginger and Curry Leaf Broth

MAKE SURE YOU HAVE PLENTY OF CRUSTY BREAD TO HELP SOAK UP
THE SPICY COCONUT AND GINGER BROTH, WHICH IS FULL OF FLAVOUR
AND WORKS EXTREMELY WELL WITH MUSSELS.

SERVES 4 | PREPARATION TIME: 20 MINUTES | COOKING TIME: 5 MINUTES

FRESH

7 garlic cloves, thinly sliced

12 fresh curry leaves

60g piece ginger, peeled and cut into julienne

about 1kg large mussels, washed, debearded and cleaned

SPICES

2 whole dried chillies

1 teaspoon ground turmeric

3 teaspoons garam masala

PANTRY/LARDER

4 tablespoons oil

100ml vegetable stock

120ml light coconut milk

salt, to taste

GARNISH

1 lime, cut into wedges

1 tablespoon finely chopped coriander

SERVE

Mint Parantha (see page 118)

1. Heat the oil in a large heavy-based saucepan over a low–medium heat. Add the dried chillies, garlic and curry leaves and fry until lightly golden.

2. Turn the heat down, add the remaining spices and stir-fry for 30 seconds.

3. Next, add the ginger and fry for a further 1 minute. Add the mussels and toss around until well coated.

4. Add the stock, coconut milk and salt to taste, cover with a lid and simmer for 3–4 minutes, or until the mussels have opened. Discard any mussels that remain closed.

5. Garnish with lime wedges and coriander and serve with Mint Parantha.

Chicken Korma

CONSIDERED TO BE A GENTLE INTRODUCTION TO INDIAN CUISINE FOR WESTERNERS, CHICKEN KORMA IS A MILD YET VERY FLAVOURSOME DISH. AS IT'S NOT SPICY, CONSIDER SERVING THIS TO CHILDREN. IT GOES WELL WITH AROMATIC RICE, SALAD AND NAAN BREAD (SEE PAGE 127).

SERVES 4–5 | PREPARATION TIME: 2 HOURS | MARINATING TIME: 2–8 HOURS
COOKING TIME: 30–60 MINUTES

FRESH
800g chicken joints
150g natural yoghurt
4 garlic cloves, very finely chopped
1 tablespoon lemon juice
2 onions, roughly chopped
5cm piece ginger, peeled and roughly chopped
1–2 small green chillies, roughly chopped

SPICES
3 bay leaves
12 green cardamom pods, cracked
½ teaspoon ground turmeric
1½ teaspoons ground coriander

PANTRY/LARDER
90ml oil
2 tablespoons cashews and 1 tablespoon white poppy seeds, soaked together in 50ml hot water
1½ teaspoons salt, or to taste
3 tablespoons double cream

GARNISH
large pinch of ground cumin

1. Make slits in each chicken joint, place in a large bowl and add 4 tablespoons of the yoghurt, 2 teaspoons of the garlic, 1 tablespoon of the oil and the lemon juice. Mix thoroughly until well coated. Cover and chill for 2 hours, or overnight.

2. In a spice grinder or blender, blitz the soaked poppy seeds and cashews with their water, then mix with the remaining yoghurt.

3. Heat the remaining oil in a large heavy-based frying pan over a medium heat. Add the onions, remaining garlic, ginger and chillies and fry until soft and golden brown. Remove with a slotted spoon and blitz together to a smooth paste.

4. Pour the paste back into the same pan, add the bay leaves and cardamom and fry together over a low–medium heat for 2–3 minutes.

5. Add the turmeric, ground coriander and salt and stir-fry for 1 minute.

6. Next, add the poppy, cashew and yoghurt paste and continue stir-frying for a further 2 minutes.

7. Add the chicken joints, stir-fry for 5–6 minutes, adding a little hot water to loosen if needed, then add the cream, cover and cook for a further 15–20 minutes, or until the chicken is cooked through.

8. Garnish with a sprinkling of ground cumin.

Classic Lamb Curry

ANOTHER FAVOURITE DISH HAILING FROM NORTH INDIA, IT IS PERFECT FOR ANY OCCASION AND HITS THE RIGHT SPOT FOR ALL CURRY LOVERS. THIS DISH IS SIMPLE, YET RICH IN FLAVOUR AND LIKE MOST CURRIES, TASTES EVEN BETTER THE NEXT DAY.

SERVES 4 | PREPARATION TIME: 30 MINUTES | COOKING TIME: 45 MINUTES

FRESH

3 onions, finely chopped

2 small green chillies

4cm piece ginger, peeled and finely grated

8 garlic cloves, finely chopped

1kg leg of lamb, chopped into 2.5cm cubes

2 tablespoons Greek-style yoghurt, whisked with 200ml water

3 tablespoons finely chopped coriander

SPICES

1 tablespoon garam masala

1½ teaspoons ground cumin, plus a large pinch for sprinkling

1½ teaspoons ground coriander

½ teaspoon chilli powder

1 tablespoon ground turmeric

PANTRY/LARDER

3 tablespoons oil

½ x 250g tin chopped tomatoes

2 teaspoons salt, or to taste

1. In a blender or using a mortar and pestle, grind the onions, green chillies, ginger, garlic, oil and tinned tomatoes into a smooth paste.

2. Mix the paste together with the garam masala, cumin, ground coriander, chilli powder, turmeric and salt. Place the lamb in a large bowl and cover in the paste, making sure all the pieces of lamb are well coated.

3. Put the lamb into a heavy-based saucepan over a low heat, cover and cook for 35–40 minutes, stirring frequently until the meat is tender and the oil has separated.

4. Add the yoghurt, then cover and cook for a further 5 minutes, stirring constantly over a low–medium heat.

5. Remove from the heat then sprinkle with the chopped coriander and a large pinch of ground cumin and serve.

Lemon and Saffron Pot Roast Chicken

A DELICIOUS, LAID-BACK KIND OF DISH BEST ENJOYED WITH FRIENDS AT LUNCH. SERVE WITH STEAMED GREEN BEANS IN TOMATO AND MUSTARD DRESSING (SEE PAGE 74), SIMPLE SALAD LEAVES AND STEAMED POTATOES.

SERVES 3–4 | PREPARATION TIME: 15 MINUTES | COOKING TIME: 1½ HOURS

FRESH

2 tablespoons grated ginger
3 garlic cloves, finely chopped
grated zest and juice of 2 lemons
1.5kg whole chicken
2 tablespoons crème fraîche

SPICES

1 tablespoon ground cumin
2 tablespoons ground coriander
5–6 saffron threads, soaked
in 1 teaspoon milk

BOUQUET GARNI

1 large cinnamon stick
2 bay leaves
3 star anise
4 cardamom pods

PANTRY/LARDER

2–3 tablespoons vegetable oil
2 teaspoons salt, or to taste

1. Preheat the oven to 170–190°C/325–375°F/Gas 3–5.

2. Place the ginger, garlic, ground cumin, ground coriander, lemon zest, lemon juice, soaked saffron threads and oil in a bowl and mix. Rub all over the whole chicken and place in a lidded ovenproof dish.

3. Add the bouquet garni spices and salt, then pour in enough water to come a third of the way up the chicken. Cover with the lid.

4. Place in the oven and cook for 1 hour, then remove the lid and cook for a further 15–25 minutes, or until the chicken is cooked through.

5. Remove the chicken from the dish, then pour half of the cooking stock into a pan and stir in the crème fraîche. Place over a low heat and simmer for about 10–15 minutes, or until the sauce has reduced by half and slightly thickened.

6. Cut the chicken into serving pieces and pour over the sauce.

NOTE: The spices can be added straight into the dish instead of making a bouquet garni.

Baked Salmon with Crème Fraîche and Coconut

A RECIPE KINDLY SHARED BY AN UNCONVENTIONAL COOK, JEEVA JEYASEELAN. THIS IS A SIMPLE PREPARATION THAT IS PACKED FULL OF FLAVOUR, BUT STILL DELICATE. THE CRÈME FRAÎCHE, LIME JUICE AND COCONUT ALL TOGETHER FORM A DELICIOUS AND LIGHT SAUCE, AND WILL WORK WELL WITH ANY FISH, EITHER FILLETS OR AS WHOLE FISH FOR MORE PEOPLE.

SERVES 2 | PREPARATION TIME: 15 MINUTES | COOKING TIME: 15 MINUTES

FRESH

1 quantity Spiced Coconut and Crème Fraîche Marinade (see page 246)

2 salmon fillets

¼ wedge of lime

PANTRY/LARDER

2 large sheets (A4-sized) of baking paper

1. Preheat the oven to 180°C/350°F/Gas 4.

2. Rub the marinade equally into the 2 pieces of salmon.

3. Place one salmon fillet on each baking paper square, then squeeze lime juice over each fish and finish off by sprinkling 2–3 teaspoons water over each fillet.

4. Bring up the sides of the paper and pinch together, then seal the edges tightly to form a loose parcel.

5. Place both salmon parcels on a baking tray and cook in the oven for 12–15 minutes depending on the thickness of your fillet.

NOTE: Open the parcels very carefully as the steam that will escape will be very hot.

Any leftovers can be made into mouth-watering fishcakes.

Lamb Kofta and Saffron Crème Fraîche

THIS IS A TRADITIONAL NORTH INDIAN DISH, USUALLY MADE WITH LAMB, BUT YOU CAN ALSO CONSIDER USING BEEF, WHICH IS EQUALLY NICE. PREPARE THE MEATBALLS AND THE SAUCE SEPARATELY THE NIGHT BEFORE. THE NEXT DAY, COMBINE AND FINISH OFF COOKING ACCORDING TO THE RECIPE. THIS DISH CAN BE EATEN AS IT IS, HOWEVER, THE DELICIOUS SAFFRON-INFUSED CRÈME FRAÎCHE GIVES THIS DISH A LUXURIOUS FINISH.

SERVES 4 | PREPARATION TIME: 2 HOURS
CHILLING TIME: 1–8 HOURS | COOKING TIME: ABOUT 1½ HOURS

FRESH

450g lamb mince

2 onions, grated and squeezed dry using a cloth or placed in a sieve, then as much liquid pressed out as possible with the back of a spoon

8 garlic cloves, very finely chopped

3 tablespoons grated ginger

4 small green chillies

4 tablespoons finely chopped coriander

SPICES

2 teaspoons cumin seeds

4 black cardamom pods, cracked

2 bay leaves

2.5cm piece cassia or cinnamon stick

1 tablespoon garam masala

1 teaspoon ground turmeric

large pinch of nutmeg

PANTRY/LARDER

2 teaspoons salt, or to taste

4 tablespoons oil

2 tablespoons tomato paste (concentrated purée) dissolved in 250ml hot water or meat stock

GARNISH

soak a tiny pinch of saffron threads in 1 tablespoon hot water, mix together with 1–2 tablespoons crème fraîche and 1 tablespoon lemon juice

1. Add the following to a large blender: lamb mince, half the onions, half the garlic, half the ginger, half the chillies, half the chopped coriander and 1 teaspoon salt and blitz together until completely smooth. You may need to stop the blender, remove the lid and move the mixture around with a spatula.

2. Put the mixture in a large bowl and, using damp hands, roll a small portion of mixture into a smooth ball. Place the balls onto a lightly oiled tray, cover with plastic wrap and refrigerate for 1–2 hours, or preferably overnight.

3. Heat the oil in a heavy-based frying pan over low–medium heat. Add the cumin, cardamom, bay leaves and cassia or cinnamon stick and fry for 20 seconds.

4. Next, reduce the heat slightly and add the remaining onions, garlic, ginger and chillies and fry for 5 minutes, or until golden brown.

5. Add the garam masala, turmeric, nutmeg and remaining salt and keep stirring and frying for 30 seconds.

6. Pour in the tomato purée and water mix, bring to a gentle simmer, then gently slip in the meatballs and continue cooking, uncovered, for a further 30–35 minutes, or until the meatballs are cooked and the sauce is thick. Drizzle with the crème fraîche garnish.

Fish in Tamarind Sauce

THE TAMARIND IN THIS GRAVY-BASED DISH GIVES IT A LOVELY TANGY
FLAVOUR THAT GOES REALLY WELL WITH SIMPLE, PLAIN BOILED RICE,
RAW SHREDDED VEGETABLE SALADS OR STEAMED GREENS.

SERVES 4–5 | PREPARATION TIME: 30 MINUTES
MARINATING TIME: 1 HOUR | COOKING TIME: 40 MINUTES

FRESH

5 x 2.5cm thick pieces of fish,
such as halibut, cod or haddock

1 quantity Coconut and Tamarind with
Red Chilli and Ground Spices Marinade
(see page 247)

8–10 fresh curry leaves

2 green chillies, slit lengthways
down the middle

2 onions, roughly chopped

3 garlic cloves and 1cm piece ginger,
mashed into a paste (see page 231)

1 large tomato, finely chopped

SPICES

1½ teaspoons black mustard seeds

½ teaspoon ground cumin

PANTRY/LARDER

3 tablespoons oil

salt and black pepper, to taste

240ml tinned coconut milk

1. Put the pieces of fish in a large, flat dish and mix in the marinade, making sure all the pieces are well coated. Cover and marinate for 1 hour.

2. Heat the oil in a deep frying pan over a medium heat until hot. Add the curry leaves, black mustard seeds and green chillies and fry until the spluttering stops.

3. Now add the onions and garlic–ginger paste and fry over a low heat until the paste begins to brown very slightly, about 6–8 minutes.

4. Add the chopped tomato and fry, stirring frequently, over a low heat for 3–4 minutes, or until the onion base starts to release its oil and turns a rich golden brown.

5. Strain the fish, then add the fish marinade to the pan and stir. Gently bring to the boil over a medium heat and add pepper and the cumin and coconut milk. Turn down the heat slightly and simmer until the oil begins to appear on top of the gravy. Add the fish now and cook for 12–15 minutes, or until the fish flakes easily with a fork. If stirring, do so very gently to avoid breaking the fish.

N O T E : If the fish has been cut into cubes then cook in the sauce for 5–6 minutes until the fish flakes easily with a fork.

Beef and Potato Curry

A SLOW-SIMMERED CURRY WITH AN INTERESTING COMBINATION OF SPICES IS JUST THE THING TO WARM YOU UP ON A WINTRY DAY. SERVE WITH WARMED NAAN BREAD (SEE PAGE 127) AND SPINACH AND MINT YOGHURT (SEE PAGE 196). THIS DISH IS PERFECT FOR MEAT LOVERS AND CAN BE ENJOYED DURING A CASUAL DINNER PARTY OR A FAMILY MEAL.

SERVES 4 | PREPARATION TIME: 35 MINUTES | COOKING TIME: 2 HOURS 10 MINUTES

FRESH

3 onions, finely chopped

8 small green chillies, finely chopped

2.5cm piece ginger, peeled and finely shredded

4 garlic cloves, very finely chopped

1kg casserole steak or stewing beef, diced into 2.5cm cubes

1 potato, peeled and chopped into large cubes

SPICES

1½ tablespoons garam masala

1 tablespoon ground turmeric

4 cloves

2 bay leaves

4 green cardamom pods, slightly cracked

5cm piece cassia or cinnamon stick or 1 teaspoon ground cinnamon

1 teaspoon fennel seeds

PANTRY/LARDER

400ml tin coconut milk

25g ground almonds

1 tablespoon tomato paste (concentrated purée)

3 tablespoons ghee or oil

2 teaspoons salt, or to taste

1. Mix together the coconut milk, ground almonds and tomato purée to form a paste. Set aside.

2. In a mini blender or using a mortar and pestle, grind the onions, green chillies, garam masala, turmeric, ginger and garlic to a smooth paste.

3. Heat the ghee or oil in a large heavy-based saucepan over a medium heat. Add the cloves, bay leaves, cardamom, cassia or cinnamon stick and fennel seeds and fry for 1 minute.

4. When they begin to crackle add the onion paste and cook over a low heat for 3–4 minutes, or until the oil separates and the paste turns golden brown.

5. Stir in the meat, turn up the heat slightly and continue cooking, stirring occasionally for 10–12 minutes, or until the liquid has evaporated and the meat starts to brown.

6. Next, stir in the coconut paste and salt, then stir well until the meat is coated. Cook for 4–5 minutes, stirring occasionally. Cover with a lid and simmer for 1 hour 15–20 minutes.

7. Add the potato, cover and continue simmering for 30 minutes, or until the meat is tender and the potato is cooked through.

8. Remove from the heat, keep covered with the lid and allow the meat to rest for 15–20 minutes before serving.

Prawn Curry

DELIGHTFUL, WITH A KICK, THIS SOUTH INDIAN PRAWN LOVER'S FAVOURITE DISH IS IDEAL FOR COLD WINTER EVENINGS OR LIGHT SUMMER SUPPERS.

SERVES 4 | PREPARATION TIME: 20 MINUTES | COOKING TIME: 15 MINUTES

FRESH
450g raw prawns
juice of 1 lime
7–8 fresh curry leaves
½ onion, finely chopped
3 garlic cloves, finely crushed
2 teaspoons grated ginger
juice of ½ lemon

SPICES
5cm piece cinnamon stick
½ teaspoon fenugreek seeds
½ teaspoon ground turmeric
1 teaspoon chilli powder

PANTRY/LARDER
3 tablespoons oil
55g creamed coconut
1 teaspoon salt, or to taste

1. Peel and devein the prawns. Put them into a bowl, add the lime juice and leave to stand for 5 minutes. Wash the prawns under cold water and pat dry with paper towel.

2. Heat the oil in a medium saucepan, then reduce the heat and add the cinnamon stick and curry leaves. Toss around for a few seconds, then add the fenugreek seeds and fry for a further 1 minute, or until the seeds are a rich dark brown.

3. Add the onion and fry over a medium heat until golden brown. Next, add the garlic and ginger and fry for a further 1 minute.

4. Turn the heat down, add the turmeric and fry for a further 1 minute. Next, add the creamed coconut, chilli powder, 125ml water and salt to taste. Bring slowly to the boil, then reduce the heat and simmer until the creamed coconut has dissolved.

5. Add the prawns, bring back to the boil, then reduce the heat and simmer for 5–7 minutes.

6. Finally, remove the pan from the heat, add the lemon juice and mix thoroughly.

NOTE: If using ready-cooked prawns, add them to the simmering sauce just prior to serving.

Butter Chicken

CREATED IN A POPULAR EATING JOINT IN THE BACK STREETS OF DELHI OVER 40 YEARS AGO, BUTTER CHICKEN NOW HAS AN ICONIC STATUS IN INDIA AS THE FAVOURITE NON-VEGETARIAN CHOICE. INDULGE YOURSELF IN THIS RICH AND FLAVOURSOME TREAT THAT GOES WELL WITH NAAN BREAD (SEE PAGE 127) AS WELL AS AROMATIC RICE.

SERVES 4 | PREPARATION TIME: 30 MINUTES | COOKING TIME: 20 MINUTES

FRESH

2 onions, roughly chopped

4 garlic cloves, roughly chopped

5cm piece ginger, peeled and roughly chopped

410g Chicken Tikka (see page 48)

2 tablespoons double cream

SPICES

2 black cardamom pods, slightly cracked

4 green cardamom pods, slightly cracked

1 teaspoon ground turmeric

½–1 teaspoon chilli powder

1 teaspoon garam masala

PANTRY/LARDER

4 tablespoons oil

1 teaspoon salt, or to taste

2 tablespoons tomato passata (puréed tomatoes)

2 tablespoons coconut milk powder

1 tablespoon ground almonds

¼ teaspoon granulated sugar

1 teaspoon ghee

NOTE

Raw chicken thighs can also be used; cover and adjust the cooking time to 20 minutes.

1. Heat 2 tablespoons of the oil in a frying pan over a medium heat. Add the onions, garlic and ginger and fry for 3–4 minutes until caramelised and a rich golden brown. Remove from the heat, cool slightly, then blitz into a smooth paste in a blender.

2. Add the remaining oil to the same pan and heat over a medium heat. Add the black and green cardamom pods and gently fry for 30 seconds, then straight away add the onion paste.

3. Turn the heat down and add the turmeric, chilli powder, garam masala and salt and stir-fry for 1 minute, then remove from the heat.

4. Next, blitz together the passata, coconut milk powder, ground almonds, sugar and 4 tablespoons water in a blender. Pour into the pan and stir. Return the pan to a low heat and cook for 3–5 minutes. Add the cooked Chicken Tikka pieces and cook through gently for 3–4 minutes. Add the double cream and cook for a further 2 minutes.

5. Finish off with a drizzle of ghee and serve with rice.

Breads
and Rice

CHAPTER 4

Mint Parantha

A REFRESHING TWIST ON THE PLAIN PARANTHA THAT
GOES WELL WITH FLAVOURED YOGHURTS, MEAT OR VEGETABLE
DISHES. AS WITH ALL PARANTHAS THEY ARE BEST EATEN HOT.

SERVES 4 | PREPARATION TIME: 45 MINUTES
COOKING TIME: 3–4 MINUTES PER PARANTHA

FRESH
50g mint leaves, finely chopped
1 quantity Plain Naan dough
(see page 127)

SPICES
2 teaspoons ground cumin
1 teaspoon ground black pepper
¼ teaspoon ajwain seeds (optional)

PANTRY/LARDER
½ teaspoon salt, or to taste
flour, for dusting
4 tablespoons melted ghee,
butter or oil
1 tablespoon dried mint

OPTIONAL GARNISH
sprinkle each mint parantha with
a small pinch of chaat masala

1. Place a flat griddle or frying pan over a low–medium heat.

2. Using a mortar and pestle, pound together the chopped mint leaves, cumin, pepper, salt and ajwain seeds, if using. Set aside.

3. Lightly dust the work surface with flour. From the naan dough, take a medium-sized ball, flatten it and dust with some flour. Using a rolling pin, roll it into a circle with a 12cm diameter. Use a brush to spread some ghee, butter or oil all over the circle, and a sprinkling of flour.

4. Take a heaped teaspoon of the mint masala and spread it all over the circle of dough.

5. Starting from one side, fold and gather the dough together like a fan, then curl up from one side and roll back into a ball. Press down and dust with flour.

6. Roll out until it becomes a large thin circle. If sticking in between, keep dusting with flour.

7. Gently lift the parantha off the surface and place onto the hot pan. Turn up the heat to medium. The parantha will soon start to puff up. After 30 seconds, flip over, brush very lightly with water and sprinkle a pinch of dried mint all over. Gently press using a palette knife, cook for 1 minute, flip again and brush with ghee, butter or oil. Flip over again and swirl the pan around for 30 seconds. Brush with more ghee, butter or oil and serve hot. Repeat with the remaining ingredients. Sprinkle with some chaat masala, if desired.

NOTE: If made in advance, gently reheat each one in a frying pan before serving.

Parantha with Ajwain, Fennel and Chilli Butter

PARANTHAS ARE USUALLY EATEN AS PART OF BREAKFAST OR BRUNCH, AND SERVED WITH MASALA SCRAMBLED EGGS (SEE PAGE 70), ACCOMPANIED BY A GLASS OF HOT MASALA CHAI (SEE PAGE 212).

MAKES 6–8 | PREPARATION TIME: 45 MINUTES
COOKING TIME: 3–4 MINUTES PER PARANTHA

FRESH
1 quantity Plain Roti dough (see page 126)

SPICES
¼ teaspoon ajwain seeds
¼ teaspoon red chilli flakes
¼ teaspoon fennel seeds

PANTRY/LARDER
½ teaspoon salt, or to taste
flour, for dusting
2 tablespoons melted ghee, for brushing

1. Place a flat griddle or frying pan over a low–medium heat.

2. Using a mortar and pestle, crush together the ajwain, fennel, red chilli flakes and salt and set aside.

3. Lightly dust the work surface with flour. From the dough, take a medium-sized ball, flatten it and dust with some flour. Using a rolling pin, roll into a circle with a 12cm diameter. Use a brush to spread some melted ghee all over the circle.

4. Take a couple of large pinches of the spice mix and sprinkle liberally all over the dough circle. Bring one side of the circle into the middle and press lightly. Spread a little ghee over the top, fold the opposite side of the rolled dough on top of the folded part, then press lightly and brush with melted ghee. Lastly, fold the top and bottom parts and brush with a little more ghee. Dust the small square with flour and roll out until it becomes a large thin square. If sticking in between, keep dusting with flour.

5. Gently lift the parantha off the surface and place onto the hot pan. Turn up the heat to medium. The parantha will soon start to puff up. After 30–60 seconds flip over and gently press with a palette knife. Cook for 1 minute, flip again and brush with ghee, then flip over again and swirl the pan around for 30 seconds. Repeat with the remaining dough and spice mix. Serve hot.

NOTE: To make plain paranthas, leave out the spice mix and use only the salt.

White Radish and Onion Parantha

THIS 'ALL-IN-ONE' BREAD TAKES SOME EFFORT AND A LITTLE SKILL, BUT THE RESULTS ARE WORTH IT. THE BREAD ENVELOPS THE SPICED DAIKON MASALA, LEAVING IT TENDER AND SWEET. PERFECT FOR BRUNCH OR A PICNIC. TRULY DELICIOUS HOT, BUT STILL FANTASTIC SERVED COLD.

MAKES 6–8 | PREPARATION TIME: 1 HOUR
COOKING TIME: 3–5 MINUTES PER PARANTHA

FRESH

230g daikon, finely shredded into long ribbons and squeezed dry using a muslin (cheese cloth) or clean tea towel

½ small red onion, finely chopped and squeezed dry using a muslin (cheese cloth) or clean tea towel

½ green chilli, finely chopped

2.5cm piece ginger, peeled and finely shredded or chopped

2 tablespoons finely chopped coriander

1 quantity Plain Roti dough (see page 126)

SPICES

½ teaspoon pomegranate seed powder

½ teaspoon ajwain seeds

1 tablespoon fenugreek leaves

1 teaspoon garam masala

1 teaspoon ground cumin

PANTRY/LARDER

flour, for dusting

1 teaspoon salt, or to taste

4 tablespoons melted ghee, butter or oil

1. Mix together the daikon, onion, chilli, ginger, coriander, pomegranate seed powder, ajwain seeds, fenugreek leaves, garam masala and ground cumin in a bowl.

2. Heat a non-stick, heavy-based frying pan or crêpe pan over a low–medium heat.

3. Divide the dough into 6–8 equal pieces, then roll the balls in the palm of your hands and flatten into small discs. Dust the discs with flour and, using a rolling pin, roll out until they become medium-sized discs. If sticking in between, keep dusting with flour.

4. Take 1 heaped tablespoon of the daikon mix and place in the middle of the discs. Sprinkle with a large pinch of salt, then bring together the sides and pinch in the middle until the mixture is completely concealed. Dust with flour, flatten and continue to gently roll out until a large thin disc. Repeat with all the discs and filling.

5. Gently lift the parantha off the surface and place onto the hot pan. Turn up the heat to medium. The parantha will soon start to puff up. After 30–60 seconds, flip over.

6. Gently press the parantha using a palette knife, cook for 1 minute and flip again. Brush with ghee, butter or oil, flip over again and swirl the pan around for 30 seconds. Repeat with the remaining paranthas. Serve hot or cold.

Cauliflower, Cumin and Spring Onion Parantha

CRISPY PARANTHA STUFFED WITH FINELY SHREDDED CAULIFLOWER, SPRING ONION AND TOASTED CUMIN IS A SUBSTANTIAL CHOICE FOR BRUNCH, LUNCH OR AS A SNACK. SERVE WITH NATURAL YOGHURT SPRINKLED WITH A PINCH OF CHAAT MASALA.

SERVES 4 | PREPARATION TIME: 1 HOUR
COOKING TIME: 3–5 MINUTES PER PARANTHA

FRESH

150g cauliflower, finely grated or blitzed in blender until fine

2 spring onions, thinly sliced

2cm piece ginger, peeled and finely grated

½ small red chilli, seeded (optional) and finely chopped

2 tablespoons finely chopped coriander

1 quantity Plain Roti dough (see page 126)

SPICES

1 teaspoom cumin seeds, toasted and finely crushed

1 teaspoon garam masala

¾ tablespoon fenugreek leaves

PANTRY/LARDER

flour, for dusting

1 teaspoon salt, or to taste

4 tablespoons melted ghee, butter or oil

1. Mix together the cauliflower, spring onions, ginger, chilli, cumin seeds, garam masala, fenugreek leaves and coriander.

2. Heat a heavy-based non-stick frying pan or crêpe pan over a low–medium heat. Divide the dough into 6–8 equal pieces, then roll the balls in the palm of your hands and flatten each one into a small disc. Dust the discs with flour and, using a rolling pin, roll out until each one becomes a medium-sized disc. If sticking in between, keep dusting with flour.

3. Take 1 heaped tablespoon of the cauliflower mixture and place in the middle of a disc, sprinkle over a little salt, then bring together the sides and pinch in the middle until the mixture is completely concealed. Dust with flour, flatten and continue to gently roll out until it is a large thin disc.

4. Gently lift the parantha off the surface and place onto the hot pan. Turn up the heat to medium. The parantha will soon start to puff up. After 30–60 seconds, flip over. Gently press the parantha using a palette knife and cook for 1 minute. Flip again and brush with ghee, butter or oil, then flip over again and swirl the pan around for 30 seconds. Repeat with the remaining dough discs. Serve hot.

HOW TO MAKE
Plain Roti

ROTI IS AN EVERYDAY INDIAN FLATBREAD, WHEREAS NAAN IS THE
MOST POPULAR FLATBREAD, ESPECIALLY OUTSIDE OF INDIA. ROTI IS THINNER,
CONTAINS NO YEAST AND IS COOKED ON A FLAT GRIDDLE PAN.

MAKES 6–8 | PREPARATION TIME: 20–25 MINUTES | RESTING TIME: 20–25 MINUTES
COOKING TIME: 2 MINUTES EACH SIDE

EQUIPMENT

LARGE BOWL
MEASURING JUG
ROLLING PIN
FLAT GRIDDLE PAN
PASTRY BRUSH

Sift

1 Sift 360g whole-wheat/ atta/chapati flour or 225g self-raising flour (plus extra for dusting) into a large bowl.

Mix

2 Drizzle 1 tablespoon oil over the flour and make a well in the centre. Using one hand, pour in 125ml cold water (or more if needed), a little at a time and with the other hand use a fork to gradually bring in the flour and mix together. Keep pouring a little water, while mixing and kneading together. Add enough water to make a soft, but not sticky dough. If it's too wet then add more flour; if too dry add more water.

Rest

3 Keep kneading for about 5 minutes, or until it is smooth, pliable and soft. The consistency should not be very soft or hard. Cover and rest for 20–25 minutes.

4 Divide the dough into 6–8 equal-sized pieces, then roll the balls in the palms of your hands. Using a rolling pin, roll each one out into a large thin disc.

Cook

Roll

5 Gently lift, and place onto a hot pan. Cook one side until under half-cooked, flip over using tongs, and cook until brown spots appear. Flip back over and finish the other side until the roti starts to puff up. Remove and brush with 1–2 tablespoons ghee or butter. Serve hot.

HOW TO MAKE

Plain Naan

NAAN IS AN UNLEAVENED BREAD MADE USING YEAST, THAT IS SOFT,
LIGHT AND TRADITIONALLY MADE IN CLAY OVENS. BOTH NAAN AND ROTI ARE
PERFECT CHOICES FOR WRAPS AND ACCOMPANIMENTS FOR CURRIES.

MAKES 7–8 | PREPARATION TIME: 1 HOUR | RESTING TIME: 20–25 MINUTES
COOKING TIME: 2–3 MINUTES EACH SIDE

EQUIPMENT

LARGE BOWL
MEASURING JUG
ROLLING PIN
BAKING TRAY
PASTRY BRUSH

1

Mix together 1 x 7g sachet dried yeast, 1 teaspoon golden caster sugar (optional) and 200ml warm water. Stir well with a fork and leave for a few minutes. Place 400g strong bread flour (plus extra for dusting), 2 tablespoons melted ghee or oil and ¼ tablespoon fine sea salt into a wide bowl and make a well in the centre.

2

Using one hand, pour in a little of the yeast mixture, and with the other hand use a fork to gradually bring the flour in and mix together. Keep pouring a little water while mixing. Flour your hands and begin to knead and form a ball. Add enough water to make a soft, but not sticky dough and keep kneading for about 5 minutes, or until smooth, pliable and soft. The consistency should not be very soft or hard. Cover and rest for 20–25 minutes.

Stir

Mix

Divide

3

Using lightly oiled hands, divide the dough into about 8–10 equal-sized balls. Place on a lightly oiled tray, leaving gaps in between each ball and cover with a damp tea towel. Leave in a warm place for about 20 minutes until the balls have doubled in size.

4

Preheat the grill to medium–high with a heavy-based baking tray placed on the top shelf. Roll out the dough balls thinly and evenly. One by one, place the rolled out naan onto the baking tray, brush lightly with water and grill for about 1–2 minutes on both sides, or until lightly browned and puffed up. Lightly brush with 2 tablespoons ghee and serve hot.

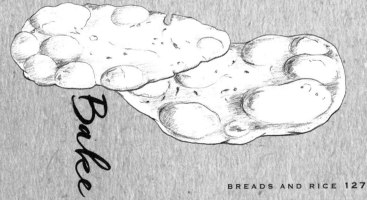

Bake

Seeded Naan Bread

THE MIXED SEEDS IN THIS RECIPE BRING THE NAAN BREAD ALIVE,
ALSO TRY KNEADING WITH BLACK POPPY SEEDS, FENUGREEK LEAVES,
DRIED FRUIT OR FINELY CHOPPED NUTS. TEARDROP/LEAF SHAPE
IS MOST COMMON, BUT ROLL OUT IN ANY SHAPE YOU LIKE.

SERVES 8–10 | PREPARATION TIME: ABOUT 1 HOUR
COOKING TIME: 4–5 MINUTES PER NAAN

FRESH
1 quantity Plain Naan dough
(see page 127)

SPICES
1 teaspoon fennel seeds
1 teaspoon caraway seeds
¼ teaspoon ajwain seeds (optional)
1½ teaspoons sesame seeds
1½ teaspoons nigella seeds

PANTRY/LARDER
melted ghee, butter or oil,
for brushing

1. Using a mortar and pestle or a rolling pin, lightly crush together the fennel seeds, caraway and ajwain seeds, if using, and add to the dry flour (see Step 1, page 127).

2. Follow all the steps for the plain naan recipe (see page 127), but just before placing under the grill, sprinkle each naan with a large pinch each of the sesame and nigella seeds. Continue as per the plain naan recipe. Brush lightly with ghee, butter or oil and serve hot.

NOTE: These naans freeze very well. Cook, but don't brush with butter or sprinkle with seeds. Freeze batches with baking paper lining in between, then place in a container. Freeze for up to a month.

Mixed Vegetable Roti

UNLIKE STUFFED PARANTHAS, THIS RECIPE SIMPLY KNEADS
TOGETHER SHREDDED VEGETABLES AND SPICES. CONSIDER USING
SHREDDED CELERY, BROCCOLI, CABBAGE, DAIKON OR POTATOES.

SERVES 6–8 | PREPARATION TIME: 1 HOUR
RESTING TIME: 20–25 MINUTES | COOKING TIME: 3–4 MINUTES PER ROTI

FRESH

1 quantity Plain Roti dough (see page 126)

115g carrot, roughly chopped

115g cauliflower, roughly chopped

100g spinach, roughly chopped

57g leek, roughly chopped

2.5cm piece ginger, peeled and roughly chopped

½ small green chilli, seeded (optional) and thinly sliced

2 tablespoons roughly chopped coriander

SPICES

½ teaspoon ajwain seeds

¼ teaspoon ground turmeric

1½ teaspoons garam masala

1 tablespoon fenugreek leaves

PANTRY/LARDER

1 teaspoon salt, or to taste

1 teaspoon sesame seeds

flour, for dusting

2 tablespoons melted ghee, for brushing

1. Place all the fresh ingredients, except for the Roti dough, into a blender and pulse until finely shredded and all mixed together.

2. Add to the Roti flour (see Step 1, page 126). Mix and massage the spices, salt and shredded vegetables with the Roti flour and sesame seeds until all the water from the vegetables has been soaked up by the flour, then gradually start adding the water (see Step 2, page 126) and bring the dough together. Keep kneading to form a soft and smooth consistency, then leave the dough to rest for 20–25 minutes.

3. Heat a heavy-based non-stick frying pan or crêpe pan over a low–medium heat. Divide the dough into 6–8 equal pieces, then roll the balls in the palms of your hands. Using a rolling pin, roll each one out into a large thin disc on the floured work surface.

4. Gently lift each disc and place onto the hot pan. Cook one side until under half-cooked, then flip over with tongs and cook until brown spots appear. Flip back over and finish cooking the other side until the roti starts to puff up. Remove from the pan and brush with ghee. Serve hot.

Onion and Coriander Stuffed Naan

SOFT NAAN BREAD STUFFED WITH ONION AND FRESH CORIANDER. EAT IT WITH MASALA-BASED DISHES, SKEWERED MEATS AND BARBECUED PANEER.

MAKES 8–10 | PREPARATION TIME: ABOUT 30 MINUTES
COOKING TIME: 4–5 MINUTES PER NAAN

FRESH

1 small red onion, finely grated and squeezed dry using a cloth or placed in a sieve, and liquid pressed out as much as possible with the back of a spoon

3–4 tablespoons finely chopped coriander

1 quantity Plain Naan dough (see page 127)

SPICES

¼ teaspoon red chilli flakes (optional)

PANTRY/LARDER

salt, or to taste

flour, for dusting

4 tablespoons melted ghee, for brushing

1. Preheat the grill to medium–high setting, with a heavy-based baking tray placed on the top shelf.

2. In a bowl, mix together the red onion, coriander, chilli flakes, if using, and salt.

3. Roll out the Naan dough balls thinly and evenly. Place a small heap of the onion and coriander mix in the centre of each one, leaving the edges free.

4. Pinch the edges together all the way around to form a pouch, then flip the pouch so the seam side is facing down on a well-floured surface. Flour the top and roll the pouch into a 3mm thick oval. Add a dusting of flour if sticking.

5. Place the rolled out naan on the baking tray, brush lightly with water and grill for about 1–2 minutes on both sides, or until lightly browned and puffed up.

6. Brush the naan with melted ghee and serve hot. Repeat with the remaining ingredients.

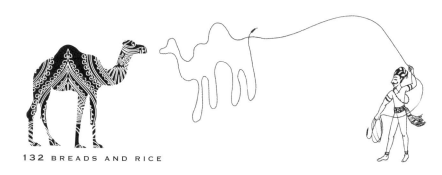

Simple Plain Rice

MAKE PERFECT WHITE RICE EVERY TIME WITH THIS RECIPE. THEN TRY
THE NEXT STEP IF YOU WISH – TEMPER THE RICE TO ADD FURTHER
FLAVOUR OR BOIL WITH A BOUQUET GARNI OR FLAVOURED STOCK.
ALWAYS CHECK IF THE RICE IS COOKED BY TESTING IT WITH A FORK.

SERVES 4 | PREPARATION TIME: 5 MINUTES | COOKING TIME: 20 MINUTES

PANTRY/LARDER

250g basmati rice,
thoroughly washed

½ teaspoon salt, or to taste

2 teaspoons ghee (optional)

1. In a medium saucepan with a tight-fitting lid, mix the rice, 500ml hot water and salt and bring to the boil. Gently stir once, cover with the lid and reduce the heat to low. Simmer for about 18 minutes.

2. Keep the lid on and remove the pan from the heat. Leave to stand, covered, for 5 minutes. Fluff up with a fork and gently stir in the ghee, if using, before serving.

NOTE: To make a different quantity of rice, always use 1 measure of uncooked rice to 2 measures of water.

Khichadi

THIS IS WHOLESOME COMFORT FOOD. A BULKED-UP VERSION OF A HUMBLE
DISH, THAT'S USUALLY EATEN MORE SOUPY, WITH ONLY A PINCH OF
SALT AND BLACK PEPPER AND NO DAIRY OR SPICES. IT IS MAINLY SERVED
TO CALM, HEAL AND SOOTHE THE DIGESTIVE SYSTEM WHEN NOT WELL.
THIS RECIPE HAS MORE OF A RISOTTO TEXTURE AS THE STOCK THAT'S
ADDED LOOSENS IT UP FOR A BROTH-LIKE CONSISTENCY.

SERVES 4 | PREPARATION TIME: 25 MINUTES | COOKING TIME: 35–40 MINUTES

FRESH

6–8 fresh curry leaves

3 garlic cloves, finely chopped

2.5cm piece ginger, peeled and finely shredded

1 onion, finely chopped

1 small green chilli, seeded (optional) and finely chopped

1 tomato, finely chopped

SPICES

¼ teaspoon ground turmeric

¾ teaspoon cumin seeds

½ teaspoon garam masala

PANTRY/LARDER

100g basmati rice, thoroughly washed

100g yellow moong dhal, thoroughly washed

1 teaspoon salt, or to taste

2 tablespoons oil

2 teaspoons ghee (optional)

1. In a large saucepan, mix the rice and dhal together and add 600ml water. Bring to the boil over a high heat, then reduce the heat to low–medium and simmer for 15 minutes. Use a large spoon to lift off any white scum or residue.

2. Add the turmeric and salt and continue to simmer over a low heat for a further 10–15 minutes, occasionally stirring and pressing the dhal and rice against the pan with the back of your spoon, until everything is soft and creamy. Add a little boiling water if it's too thick. Turn off the heat.

3. In a frying pan, heat the oil over a medium heat. Add the curry leaves and cumin seeds, then as soon as they start to crackle add the garlic and ginger and stir-fry for 30 seconds.

4. Add the onion and fry until soft and golden, then add the garam masala and green chilli and fry for 1 minute. Add the tomato and fry for 30 seconds.

5. Add the fried mixture to the cooked dhal and rice, then gently stir and cook all together for a further 5–8 minutes over a low heat. Serve with a drizzle of ghee, if liked.

Coconut Rice

FOR THOSE WHO LIKE THE RICH, CREAMY FLAVOUR OF COCONUTS, THIS DISH ADDS ANOTHER DIMENSION TO ENJOYING RICE. IT IS FULL OF TEXTURE, BUT CAN BE DRY, SO SERVE WITH SAUCE-BASED CURRIES.

SERVES 4 | PREPARATION TIME: 10 MINUTES | COOKING TIME: 5–7 MINUTES

FRESH
8–10 fresh curry leaves

85g grated fresh coconut or desiccated coconut

1 quantity cooked Simple Plain Rice (see page 134)

SPICES
1 teaspoon mustard seeds

1cm piece cassia or cinnamon stick

5–6 green cardamom pods, lightly crushed

1 whole dried chilli

PANTRY/LARDER
1 tablespoon coconut oil or oil

salt, to taste (optional)

2 teaspoons ghee (optional)

GARNISH
crushed mixed seeds and nuts, such as pistachios, almonds, cashews, peanuts and sesame seeds, gently roasted in a non-stick pan over a low heat until golden, then cooled and crushed until coarse with a rolling pin

1. Heat the oil in a frying pan over a low–medium heat. Add the mustard seeds, cassia or cinnamon stick, cardamom pods, dried chilli and curry leaves and fry gently for 20 seconds.

2. Next, add the coconut and salt, if using, and cook for a further 3–4 minutes.

3. Combine this mixture with the cooked rice, garnish with crushed mixed nuts and drizzle with ghee, if liked.

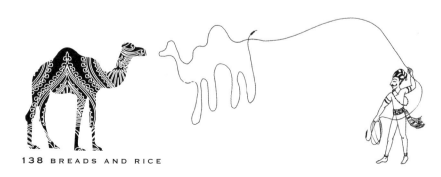

Whole Spice, Crispy Onion and Lentil Rice

WITH THEIR UNIQUE PEPPERY FLAVOUR, PUY LENTILS MAKE THIS
RICE DISH FABULOUS. THE SHAPE OF THE PUY LENTILS HOLDS
DURING COOKING AND COMBINES SUPERBLY WITH THE SPICES.
MAKE SURE THE LENTILS ARE COOKED AL DENTE.

SERVES 4 | PREPARATION TIME: 15 MINUTES | COOKING TIME: 20–25 MINUTES

FRESH

1cm piece ginger, peeled
and finely grated

1 quantity cooked Simple Plain Rice
(see page 134)

SPICES

1 black cardamom pod

½ teaspoon grated nutmeg

1cm piece cassia or cinnamon stick

2 cloves

½ teaspoon ground turmeric

PANTRY/LARDER

200g Puy lentils (or tiny blue-green
lentils), thoroughly washed

200ml chicken or vegetable stock

1½ teaspoons ghee or butter

¼ teaspoon salt (optional)

GARNISH

Crispy Ginger, Onion and
Garlic (see page 238)

4–5 coriander sprigs, roughly torn

1. In a medium saucepan over a medium heat, mix the lentils, stock, black cardamom pod, nutmeg, cassia or cinnamon stick, cloves and turmeric together and bring to the boil. Gently stir once, cover with a lid and reduce the heat to low.

2. Simmer for about 20–25 minutes. The lentils should be al dente and not mushy. Once cooked, stir in the grated ginger and ghee or butter and salt, if using, then mix together gently with the cooked rice.

3. Garnish with Crispy Ginger, Onion and Garlic and the torn coriander.

Vegetable Rice

IF YOU ARE LONGING FOR A COMFORTING AND SIMPLE MEAL AT
SUPPERTIME WITH NO FUSS BUT LOTS OF FLAVOUR AND GOODNESS, THEN
TRY THIS RICE DISH. FOR EXTRA DEPTH AND TEXTURE, DURING COOKING
ADD A HANDFUL OF COOKED LENTILS OR BEANS.

SERVES 2 AS A MAIN OR 4 AS A SIDE | PREPARATION TIME: 35 MINUTES
COOKING TIME: 15 MINUTES

FRESH

½ onion, finely chopped

2 small green chillies, split
lengthways down the middle

¼ cauliflower, cut into small
florets and steamed

100g cooked peas

1 potato, finely
diced and steamed

1 carrot, finely
diced and steamed

2 large tomatoes, seeded
and finely diced

1cm piece ginger, peeled
and cut into julienne

1 quantity cooked Simple Plain Rice
(see page 134), cooked with 1 x Eight
Whole Spice Bouquet Garni
(see page 248) or add individually

1 tablespoon lime juice

2 tablespoons finely
chopped coriander

SPICES

½ teaspoon cumin seeds

¼ teaspoon ground turmeric

PANTRY/LARDER

1 tablespoon oil

¼ teaspoon salt, or to taste

1 tablespoon ghee, for drizzling

1. Heat the oil in a large frying pan over a medium heat.
Add the cumin seeds and once they start to crackle add the
onion and green chillies and fry until lightly golden brown.

2. Reduce the heat slightly, add the turmeric and salt and
fry for 1 minute. Stir in the cooked vegetables and fry,
stirring, for 1–2 minutes.

3. Next, add the tomatoes and ginger and fry for 20 seconds,
then add the cooked rice and lime juice. Stir through gently
and serve with a drizzle of ghee and the chopped coriander.

Tamarind Rice

TAMARIND RICE IS QUITE POSSIBLY THE MOST COMMON AND POPULAR
ACCOMPANIMENT TO SOUTH INDIAN MEALS, OR EVEN BAKED CHICKEN
AND FISH. THE TANGY, SWEET/SPICY AND STICKY DRESSING CAN BE
MADE IN ADVANCE, AND USED TO LIVEN UP ANY LEFTOVER RICE.

SERVES 4 | PREPARATION TIME: 25 MINUTES | COOKING TIME: 45 MINUTES

FRESH
9–10 fresh curry leaves
1 small onion, finely chopped
1 quantity cooked Simple Plain Rice
(see page 134)

SPICES
½ teaspoon fennel seeds
2 dried red chillies
1 teaspoon black mustard seeds
1 teaspoon asafoetida
¼ teaspoon ground turmeric

PANTRY/LARDER
1 tablespoon chana dhal
1 tablespoon tamarind pulp
½ teaspoon soft brown sugar
½ teaspoon salt, or to taste
2 tablespoons oil

GARNISH
crushed mixed seeds and nuts, such
as cashews, peanuts and sesame seeds,
gently roasted in a non-stick pan over a
low heat until golden, then cooled and
crushed until coarse with a rolling pin

1. In a non-stick frying pan over a low–medium heat,
dry-roast the following until light golden brown: chana dhal,
fennel seeds, curry leaves, dried chillies and mustard seeds,
then cool and grind into a fine powder. Mix together the
tamarind pulp, sugar, salt and 125ml water in a bowl.

2. Heat the oil in a large frying pan over a low–medium heat,
add the onion and cook, stirring frequently until soft and
golden. Add the asafoetida, turmeric and spice powder and
fry together, while stirring for 30 seconds. Add the tamarind
pulp mixture and cook over a low heat for 10–12 minutes, or
until thick. Stir in the cooked rice, remove from the heat and
garnish with the crushed mixed nuts and seeds.

NOTE: Rice should be cooled once cooked. If you need
to make a different quantity of rice, always use 1 measure
of uncooked rice to 2 measures of water.

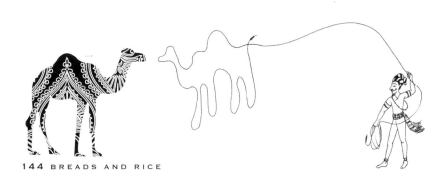

Lemon and Chickpea Rice

A FANTASTIC COMBINATION OF RICE AND CHICKPEAS CAN BE ENJOYED ON ITS OWN OR WITH A CURRY. THE CHICKPEAS ARE HIGHLY NUTRITIOUS AND PROVIDE A GOOD SOURCE OF PROTEIN IF YOU ARE A VEGETARIAN.

SERVES 4 | PREPARATION TIME: 15 MINUTES | COOKING TIME: 25 MINUTES

FRESH

zest (cut into thin strips) and juice of 1½ lemons

5cm piece ginger, peeled and cut into julienne

3 tablespoons finely chopped coriander

SPICES

1 tablespoon mustard seeds

1 tablespoon cumin seeds

1 dried red chilli

¼ teaspoon ground turmeric

PANTRY/LARDER

250g basmati rice

1 teaspoon salt, or to taste

2 tablespoons oil

180g cooked chickpeas

OPTIONAL GARNISH

Curry Leaves, Garlic, Ginger and Red Chilli (see page 240)

4 tablespoons roasted peanuts, lightly crushed

1. Pour the rice into 500ml boiling water, together with ½ teaspoon of the salt and the zest from ½ a lemon and cook for 10 minutes, then drain.

2. Heat the oil in a small frying pan over a medium heat. Add the mustard seeds and cumin seeds and as they begin to pop, turn the heat down.

3. Add the ginger and dried red chilli and fry for 30 seconds. Then add the chickpeas together with the turmeric, the remaining lemon zest and remaining salt and cook for 1 minute.

4. Add the drained rice to the pan and stir in the chopped coriander and lemon juice. Garnish, if liked.

NOTE: Shop-bought roasted peanuts work well.

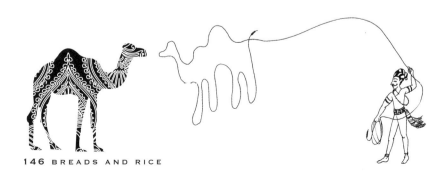

Crab-fried Rice

INSPIRED BY SOUTH INDIAN FLAVOURS, THIS SWEET, SOUR AND ZESTY
RICE DISH IS A DREAM FOR EVERY SEAFOOD LOVER. MAKE SURE
THE RICE HAS COMPLETELY COOLED DOWN BEFORE RE-USING HERE, OR
ALTERNATIVELY BEEN MADE EARLIER AND KEPT IN THE REFRIGERATOR.

SERVES 2 AS A MAIN OR 4 AS A SIDE | PREPARATION TIME: 20 MINUTES
COOKING TIME: 15 MINUTES

FRESH

1 tablespoon tamarind pulp

8–10 fresh curry leaves

½ onion, finely chopped

1 celery stick, finely chopped

3 garlic cloves, finely chopped

1cm piece ginger, peeled
and finely shredded

3 red chillies, seeded (optional)
and thinly sliced

150g crabmeat

2 tablespoons finely
chopped coriander

juice of ½ lemon or lime

1 quantity cooked Simple Plain Rice
(see page 134), preferably
cooked the night before

SPICES

1 teaspoon cumin seeds

2 teaspoons black mustard seeds

3 teaspoons fennel seeds

1 teaspoon ground turmeric

2 teaspoons garam masala

PANTRY/LARDER

1 tablespoon coconut milk powder

¼ teaspoon granulated sugar

1 teaspoon salt, or to taste

3–4 tablespoons oil

GARNISH

4–5 coriander sprigs

4 spring onions, sliced

ghee or sour cream, for drizzling

1. Mix the tamarind pulp, coconut milk powder, sugar and salt together, then set aside.

2. Heat the oil in a large frying pan over a low–medium heat. Add the cumin, mustard and fennel seeds and fry for 20–30 seconds, then add the curry leaves.

3. Add the onion and celery and fry for 2 minutes until lightly golden. Next, add the garlic, ginger and chillies and fry over a medium heat for 1 minute.

4. Add the turmeric and garam masala and fry for 1 minute. Reduce the heat, pour in the tamarind mix and gently simmer for about 2–3 minutes.

5. Stir in the crabmeat and the chopped coriander, lemon or lime juice and cooked rice and fry until the rice is fluffy and toasted.

6. Garnish with sliced spring onions, coriander and a drizzle of ghee or sour cream. Serve immediately.

Saffron and Cashew Rice

A FRAGRANT RICE THAT GOES PARTICULARLY WELL WITH MEAT AND FISH
DISHES AND IS TRADITIONALLY SERVED AS PART OF INDIAN FESTIVAL
MEALS. THE SUBTLE TASTE OF SAFFRON AND THE CRUNCHY CASHEWS
MAKE IT A LOVELY TREAT AT A DINNER PARTY OR ANY SPECIAL OCCASION.

SERVES 4 | PREPARATION TIME: 10 MINUTES | COOKING TIME: 20 MINUTES

SPICES

2.5cm piece cassia or cinnamon stick

1 star anise

2–3 cloves

6–8 small green cardamom pods,
slightly crushed

2–3 saffron threads, soaked
in 1 teaspoon milk

PANTRY/LARDER

2 tablespoons ghee or oil

2 tablespoons cashews, soaked in
a pinch of ground turmeric and hot water

250g basmati rice,
thoroughly washed

½ teaspoon salt, or to taste

1. Heat 1 tablespoon of the ghee or oil in a heavy-based saucepan with a tight-fitting lid over a low–medium heat. Add the drained cashews and gently fry for 20 seconds.

2. Add the cassia or cinnamon stick, star anise, cloves and cardamom pods and continue to fry for 30 seconds.

3. Add the rice, stir gently to coat, then add 500ml hot water, the salt and saffron threads, including the soaking milk, and bring to the boil. Gently stir once, cover with the lid and reduce the heat to low.

4. Simmer for about 18 minutes. Keep the lid on and remove the pan from the heat. Leave to stand, covered, for 5 minutes. Fluff up with a fork and gently stir in the remaining ghee or oil, if liked.

NOTE: If you need to make a different quantity of rice, use 1 measure of uncooked rice to 2 measures of water.

Chicken Pulao

WONDERFUL, SIMPLE AND SATISFYING, CHICKEN PULAO NEVER FAILS TO IMPRESS AT A CASUAL LUNCH WITH FRIENDS OR A FAMILY DINNER. UNLIKE A BIRYANI WHERE THE MEAT AND RICE ARE COOKED SEPARATELY, IN A PULAO DISH THE RICE AND MEAT OR VEGETABLES ARE COOKED TOGETHER IN ONE POT.

SERVES 4 | PREPARATION TIME: 35 MINUTES | COOKING TIME: 1 HOUR

FRESH

6 garlic cloves

2.5cm piece ginger

2 tablespoons natural yoghurt

½ large onion, thinly sliced

1kg skinless chicken on the bone, cut into pieces

2 tablespoons finely chopped coriander

SPICES

6 cloves

5cm piece cassia or cinnamon stick

4 bay leaves

2 black cardamom pods

6–8 green cardamom pods

1 tablespoon garam masala

1 teaspoon ground cumin, plus extra for sprinkling

1 teaspoon paprika

1 teaspoon chilli powder

1 teaspoon ground turmeric

PANTRY/LARDER

450ml vegetable or chicken stock or water

2 teaspoons salt, or to taste

3 tablespoons oil

250g basmati rice, thoroughly washed

SERVE

1 lime, cut into wedges

NOTE

Chicken on the bone releases a more intense flavour to the dish.

1. Using a mortar and pestle, make a fine paste with the garlic and ginger. Set aside.

2. In a small bowl, mix together the yoghurt and stock or water. Set aside.

3. Heat the oil in a large heavy-based frying pan over a low heat. Add the whole spices and fry for 20 seconds, then add the onion and fry for 20 minutes, or until golden brown. Turn up the heat, then add the ginger and garlic paste and fry for 1–2 minutes.

4. Add the chicken, ground spices and salt and mix together well. Cover with a lid and cook for 8–10 minutes, stirring occasionally.

5. Add half the yoghurt stock, stir through, bring to the boil, cover and cook for a further 10 minutes, stirring occasionally.

6. Now add the rice and coriander and the remaining yoghurt stock. Bring to the boil, then reduce the heat, cover with a lid and cook for 16–18 minutes, or until the rice liquid has evaporated and the chicken and rice are tender. Remove from the heat and leave to rest for 5–7 minutes with the lid on. Sprinkle with ground cumin and serve immediately with lime wedges.

Lamb Biryani

THIS IS A COMPLETE, 'BOWL ONLY'-STYLE SUPPER. MAKING BIRYANI IS TIME-CONSUMING BUT THE END RESULT – THE TEXTURE AND WONDERFUL FLAVOURS AND AROMAS – WILL MAKE IT WELL WORTH IT. ALTERNATIVELY, PREPARE ONLY THE FRAGRANT, LAMB MASALA THE DAY BEFORE, AND LAYER WITH COOKED RICE ONCE IT'S READY TO SERVE.

SERVES 4–5 | PREPARATION TIME: 3–4 HOURS | COOKING TIME: 1 HOUR

FRESH

1½ onions

6 garlic cloves

4cm piece ginger

2 green chillies

100g tinned chopped tomatoes

1kg boneless lamb, cut into cubes

1 quantity Simple Plain Rice (see page 134)

SPICES

4 green cardamom pods, slightly cracked

2 black cardamom pods, slightly cracked

6 cloves

4 bay leaves

1½ teaspoons cumin seeds

4cm piece cassia or cinnamon stick

2½ teaspoons garam masala

large pinch of saffron threads, soaked in 50ml warm milk

PANTRY/LARDER

1 tablespoon desiccated coconut

3 tablespoons ghee or oil

2 teaspoons salt, or to taste

GARNISH

Crispy Ginger, Onion and Garlic (see page 238)

1 teaspoon melted ghee

1. Blitz together the onions, garlic, ginger, chillies, tomatoes and desiccated coconut in a blender until they form a smooth paste.

2. In a large saucepan with a lid, heat the ghee or oil over a low–medium heat, then add all the whole spices and fry for 20 seconds, or until golden.

3. Add the lamb and coconut paste, stir until everything is coated, then cover with the lid and cook for 25 minutes over a low heat. Uncover and cook for a further 20 minutes, stirring frequently.

4. Once the oil has separated, the sauce has thickened and the lamb is cooked and tender, add the garam masala and salt. Stir and cook for 2 minutes, then turn off the heat.

5. Next, make the Simple Plain Rice according to the recipe on page 134, then drain.

6. Immediately assemble the biryani. Spread a large spoonful of rice over the base of a pan with a lid. Next, spread a layer of cooked lamb and alternate with the rice and lamb until you finish with a layer of rice.

7. Lastly, drizzle the saffron milk all over the layered biryani, cover and seal with foil. Place the lid on top and cook over a very low heat for 10 minutes. Garnish with Crispy Ginger, Onion and Garlic and a drizzle of ghee.

NOTE: Heat the lamb thoroughly, before layering with the rice. Reduce the Step 7 cooking time by 1 minute.

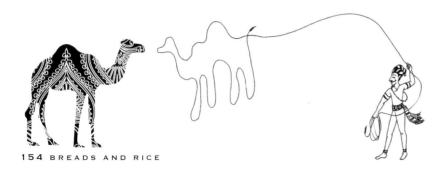

SIX
Potatoes

1 SPICY SWEET POTATO WEDGES

PREHEAT the oven to 180°C/350°F/Gas 4.

CUT 2 large unpeeled sweet potatoes into wedges and place on a heavy-based baking tray.

CRUSH 1 teaspoon fennel seeds, 1 teaspoon cumin seeds, ½–1 teaspoon red chilli flakes and 1 teaspoon salt, or to taste using a mortar and pestle.

MIX with 2 tablespoons oil. Scatter in 3 garlic cloves, lightly crushed with skins on, and toss everything together.

ROAST for 30–45 minutes, turning once.

2 MUMBAI ALOO

HEAT 3 tablespoons oil.

ADD 1 teaspoon cumin seeds and 1 teaspoon mustard seeds and after 3–4 seconds add 500g diced cooked potato and 1cm piece peeled and grated ginger, ½ teaspoon ground turmeric, 1 teaspoon ground coriander, ½ teaspoon red chilli flakes, ½ teaspoon dry mango powder (amchoor) and ½ teaspoon salt.

GENTLY keep tossing together and at the same time crushing the odd potato with the back of a fork for 6–8 minutes.

GARNISH with 2 tablespoons finely chopped coriander and a large pinch of chaat masala.

3 POTATO, PEAS AND TOMATO

HEAT 2 tablespoons oil in a frying pan over a low heat.

ADD 1 bay leaf, 1 teaspoon cumin seeds, 2 finely chopped garlic cloves and 1cm piece peeled and grated ginger.

MIX 2 tablespoons Caramelised Onion Paste (see page 231), 1 tablespoon tamarind extract and 2 tablespoons tomato passata (puréed tomatoes); pour the mixture into the pan.

FRY for 2 minutes, add 1 teaspoon ground turmeric, 1 teaspoon garam masala, 1 teaspoon ground coriander and 1½ teaspoons salt.

STIR and cook for 1 minute.

ADD 100g frozen peas and fry for 1 minute, then add 250g diced cooked potato and cook all together stirring constantly for 3–4 minutes.

REMOVE from the heat and stir in 2 finely chopped fresh tomatoes.

4 CRUSHED POTATOES

PLACE 500g peeled and chopped potatoes, together with a Three Whole Spice Bouquet Garni of crushed spices (see page 248) and 2 teaspoons salt in a large saucepan of water.

BOIL for about 8–10 minutes depending on size of the cubes. Once cooked through, drain and reserve.

HEAT 1 tablespoon oil or ghee in a small frying pan, add ½ teaspoon cumin seeds and gently fry for 20 seconds.

ADD 55g finely chopped leek (white part only) and 1½ finely chopped garlic cloves and fry for 30 seconds over a low heat until caramelised.

POUR in 25ml coconut milk. Add to the potatoes, mix and mash everything together.

DRIZZLE with ghee or butter.

GARNISH with finely chopped coriander.

5 STUFFED POTATO AND PEA CAKES

PULSE 85g peas, 25g paneer, 1 teaspoon grated ginger, ½ green chilli, ¼ teaspoon dry mango powder (amchoor), ¼ teaspoon garam masala, ¼ teaspoon salt and 1 tablespoon chopped coriander in a blender.

MIX 500g mashed potatoes, 1 teaspoon ground cumin, 1 teaspoon ground coriander, 1 teaspoon ground fennel, large pinch of chilli powder, ¼ teaspoon ground ginger, ½ teaspoon chaat masala, 1 teaspoon salt and 2 tablespoons cornflour together.

STIR together to mix. Oil your hands, take a heaped tablespoonful of the potato mix and place in the palm of your hand. Flatten and place 2 teaspoonfuls of the paneer and pea mix in the middle. Fold in all the sides and roll into a ball then flatten slightly. Repeat.

HEAT 100ml oil in a frying pan. Fry 2–3 cakes at a time for 2–3 minutes on both sides until golden brown.

6 FIVE-SPICED POTATO SALAD

HEAT 4 tablespoons oil in a heavy-based frying pan over a medium heat.

ADD 1 teaspoon panch phoran, then after about a minute of stirring add 500g halved, baby potatoes. Next, add 1 teaspoon ground turmeric, 1½ teaspoons garam masala or ground cinnamon (optional), 1 teaspoon red chilli flakes and sea salt, to taste.

FRY and keep stirring for 2 minutes. Pour in 25ml water, cover and simmer over a low heat for 8–10 minutes. Remove the lid, turn up the heat and cook, stirring until the water has completely evaporated and the potatoes are cooked through and starting to sizzle and fry.

REMOVE from the heat and gently stir in 2 finely chopped tomatoes and 1 tablespoon each of finely chopped fresh mint and coriander.

GARNISH with whole coriander and mint leaves.

Salads

Shredded Raw Veg Salad with Spice Dressing and Nuts

THIS SALAD COMPRISES DELICATE SLIVERS OF FRESH VEGETABLES,
BOLDLY TEMPERED WITH MUSTARD SEEDS, GINGER, CHILLI AND LEMON.

SERVES 2 AS A MAIN OR 4 AS A SIDE | PREPARATION TIME: 20 MINUTES
COOKING TIME: 5 MINUTES

FRESH

1 bunch of radishes, thinly sliced

2 carrots, thinly sliced

2 zucchini (courgettes), cut into thin slices or ribbons

¼ daikon, cut into thin slices or ribbons

3 spring onions, finely shredded

4–5 fresh curry leaves

juice of ¼ lemon

5mm piece ginger, peeled and finely grated

SPICES

¼ teaspoon white or black mustard seeds

large pinch of red chilli flakes

PANTRY/LARDER

1 tablespoon olive oil

salt, to taste

OPTIONAL GARNISH

1 tablespoon Mixed Nuts and Seeds (see page 240), lightly crushed

5 coriander sprigs, cut in half

1. Place all the vegetables in a large bowl.

2. Heat the oil in a small frying pan over a low heat. Add the mustard seeds and curry leaves and fry for 20 seconds. Turn off the heat.

3. Then squeeze in the lemon juice and add the red chilli flakes, ginger and salt. Pour over the vegetables and gently toss together.

4. Garnish with the crushed mixed nuts and seeds, and finish off with a scattering of coriander sprigs.

Kale, Chickpea, Mint and Preserved Lemon Salad

A REFRESHING AND HEALTHY SALAD MADE SUBSTANTIAL BY THE
ADDITION OF CHICKPEAS. IT IS ALSO SUITABLE AS A SIDE DISH, OR ENJOY
ON ITS OWN WITH BARBECUED SLICES OF PANEER OR HALOUMI.

SERVES 2 AS A MAIN OR 4 AS A SIDE | PREPARATION TIME: 20–25 MINUTES

FRESH

1 garlic clove, finely crushed

½ teaspoon finely shredded
mint leaves

2 teaspoons lemon juice

150g kale, finely shredded

1 tablespoon preserved lemon rind,
thinly sliced

SPICES

¼ teaspoon cumin seeds and
¼ teaspoon fennel seeds, lightly
toasted and crushed

¼ teaspoon red chilli flakes (optional)

PANTRY/LARDER

1 tablespoon oil

salt, to taste

180g cooked chickpeas, lightly
crushed with the back of a fork

1. Whisk together the oil, crushed spices, garlic, mint, red chilli flakes, if using, lemon juice and salt to taste.

2. Place the chickpeas and kale together in a large bowl.

3. Pour over the dressing and scatter with the preserved lemon.

Tomato and Pickled Ginger Side Salad

THIS IS A JUICY AND EFFORTLESS TOMATO SALAD, WHICH WORKS REALLY WELL WITH JAPANESE PICKLED GINGER AND THE STICKY, SWEET, SOUR CHAAT MASALA AND BALSAMIC DRESSING.

SERVES 4 AS A SIDE | PREPARATION TIME: 20 MINUTES

FRESH

8 tomatoes, halved, sliced or cut into quarters

3 teaspoons Japanese pickled ginger, finely shredded

SPICES

1 teaspoon chaat masala

¼ teaspoon red chilli flakes

PANTRY/LARDER

1½ tablespoons oil

3 teaspoons balsamic vinegar

salt, to taste

OPTIONAL GARNISH

2 teaspoons finely torn coriander leaves

¼ teaspoon nigella seeds

1. Place the tomatoes and pickled ginger in a large bowl.

2. Whisk together the oil, vinegar, chaat masala, red chilli flakes and salt to taste.

3. Pour the dressing over the tomatoes, then using your hands, toss and coat very gently.

4. Garnish with coriander and nigella seeds.

Avocado, Sweetcorn, Chilli and Coriander Salad

SERVE WITH THINLY SLICED GRIDDLED BREAD AND ENJOY AS A MAIN MEAL OR SERVE ALONGSIDE GRILLED FISH, COOKED MEATS AND PASTRIES.

SERVES 2 AS A MAIN OR 4 AS A SIDE | PREPARATION TIME: 20 MINUTES
COOKING TIME: 30 MINUTES

FRESH

2–3 whole corn-on-the-cobs

½ lime, cut into wedges

3 firm, ripe avocados, thinly sliced or cubed

½ red onion, thinly sliced

1 tablespoon roughly chopped coriander

½ large red chilli, seeded (optional) and finely chopped

1 garlic clove, very finely chopped

SPICES

¼ teaspoon cumin seeds, toasted and lightly crushed

PANTRY/LARDER

1 tablespoon melted butter

salt and black pepper, to taste

1 tablespoon oil

2 teaspoons balsamic vinegar

1. Steam the corn-on-the-cobs for about 15–17 minutes.

2. Preheat the grill to a hot setting. Brush the cobs with the melted butter and place under the hot grill. Cook, turning frequently until lightly toasted.

3. Rub the corn-on-the-cobs all over with lime wedges, then remove the kernels by sliding down the sides with a sharp knife.

4. Place the avocados, sweetcorn, reserving a little for the garnish, onion, chopped coriander and chilli into a large bowl and season with salt and pepper to taste.

5. Whisk together the oil, vinegar, garlic and crushed cumin, reserving a pinch for the garnish, and pour over the sweetcorn salad. Mix well until everything is coated with the dressing.

6. Garnish with the reserved toasted sweetcorn and toasted cumin.

Bean and Lentil Salad with Garlic and Ginger

A HEALTHY AND NOURISHING MIXTURE OF MUNG BEANS, GREEN LENTILS, BROWN LENTILS AND CHICKPEAS, FRIED TOGETHER WITH SLIVERS OF GARLIC UNTIL CRISPY AND NUTTY, FINISHED OFF WITH CARROT, GINGER AND SLICED RED ONION. THIS CAN BE SERVED WARM.

SERVES 2 AS A MAIN OR 4 AS A SIDE | PREPARATION TIME: 15 MINUTES
COOKING TIME: 15 MINUTES

FRESH

3 garlic cloves, very thinly sliced

400g mixed sprouted beans and lentils

2 large carrots, sliced into thin ribbons

4–5 chicory leaves (optional)

¼ red onion, thinly sliced

5–6 coriander sprigs, cut in half

5mm piece ginger, peeled and finely shredded

SPICES

¼ teaspoon ground coriander

¼ teaspoon ground cumin

½ teaspoon red chilli flakes

PANTRY/LARDER

2 tablespoons oil, plus extra for drizzling (optional)

salt, to taste

1. Heat the oil in a large frying pan over a low heat. Add the garlic and fry for 20 seconds.

2. Stir in the sprouted beans, together with the ground spices, chilli flakes and salt. Keep tossing and frying for 6–7 minutes, or until crispy and nutty to taste. Turn off the heat and leave to cool.

3. Place the carrots, chicory leaves, if using, onion, coriander and ginger in a bowl, then add the toasted sprouted beans and mix together well. Drizzle with oil, if needed. Serve.

Pickles and Chutneys

Coriander and Peanut Chutney

VIBRANT AND ZESTY, THIS GREEN CHUTNEY TAKES JUST MINUTES TO MAKE – ESPECIALLY IF USING SHOP-BOUGHT ROASTED PEANUTS. SERVE WITH SESAME AND GINGER CHICKEN SKEWERS (SEE PAGE 40) OR STEAK AND OTHER COOKED MEATS, NAAN BREADS (SEE PAGE 127) AND RICE.

SERVES 4 | PREPARATION TIME: 15 MINUTES

FRESH

130g coriander, roughly chopped including stalks

1 small green chilli

4 tablespoons lemon juice

PANTRY/LARDER

50g dry-roasted peanuts, crushed using a mortar and pestle or with a rolling pin until fine

3 teaspoons soft brown sugar

½ teaspoon salt, or to taste

NOTE

Shop-bought peanuts work perfectly well.

Place all the ingredients plus 1 tablespoon water in a small blender and blitz until smooth.

Raw Mango, Apple, Coriander and Mint Relish

THIS IS A TERRIFIC COMBINATION OF INGREDIENTS THAT RESULTS IN A REFRESHING AND PERKY MIX OF SWEET, SOUR AND CHILLI. THIS RELISH IS MOSTLY EATEN WITH FRITTERS, PASTRIES AND PANEER-BASED SNACKS.

SERVES 4 | PREPARATION TIME: 20 MINUTES

FRESH

1 small raw green mango, stoned and roughly chopped

½ green eating apple, cored, peeled and roughly chopped

¼ red onion, roughly chopped

1 spring onion, roughly chopped

50g coriander, roughly chopped

50g mint, roughly chopped

1 small green chilli, roughly chopped

SPICES

½ teaspoon pomegranate seed powder

1 teaspoon chaat masala

PANTRY/LARDER

¼ teaspoon soft brown sugar

¼ teaspoon salt, or to taste

Place all the ingredients in a blender and blitz until fine, but still coarse.

Fresh Tomato, Date and Tamarind Relish

THIS IS A FRESH, CLEAN-TASTING RELISH THAT HAS A REMARKABLE FRUITY, SOUR AND CHILLI EDGE. FOR BEST RESULTS, USE GOOD-QUALITY TOMATOES AND SERVE WITH BARBECUED MEATS, PANEER, SAVOURY FRITTERS AND PASTRIES.

SERVES 4 | PREPARATION TIME: 15 MINUTES

FRESH

215g (about 2 medium) fresh tomatoes, peeled and seeded

1 small green chilli

1 garlic clove

1cm piece ginger, peeled and grated

1 tablespoon finely chopped coriander

6 tablespoons tamarind pulp

SPICES

½ teaspoon ground coriander

½ teaspoon toasted cumin seeds (see Note)

PANTRY/LARDER

115g pitted dried dates, soaked in 500ml hot water until soft and plump

¼ teaspoon salt, or to taste

NOTE: To toast the cumin seeds: Place the seeds in a non-stick frying pan over a medium heat, gently tossing for 30 seconds until dark brown. Remove immediately and crush using a mortar and pestle or a rolling pin.

1. Place all the ingredients in a small blender, including the date water, and pulse gently until roughly blended.

2. Place in a clean screw-top jar, seal and refrigerate for up to 3 days.

NOTE: This relish freezes very well. It can be kept frozen for 4–5 months. Thaw before use.

Garlic and Red Chilli Chutney

NOT ONLY CAN YOU ENJOY THIS AS A CHUTNEY, BUT ALSO AS A
PASTE IN COOKING – ADD TO SOUPS, MARINADES AND OTHER
SAUCE-BASED DISHES TO BRING THEM ALIVE. THIS IS USUALLY EATEN
IN SMALL QUANTITIES, BUT IF RAW GARLIC IS TOO STRONG AND
NOT TO YOUR TASTE, ROAST THE GARLIC CLOVES FIRST, THEN
BLEND WITH THE REST OF THE INGREDIENTS.

MAKES 4–6 TABLESPOONS | PREPARATION TIME: 10 MINUTES

FRESH

1 garlic bulb, cloves peeled and
very finely chopped or crushed

2–3 teaspoons lemon juice

SPICES

3 teaspoons chilli powder, preferably
Kashmiri chilli powder

PANTRY/LARDER

3–4 tablespoons oil

½ teaspoon salt, or to taste

Place all the fresh ingredients and spices in a
blender with half the oil and the salt and blitz,
then add the remaining oil and continue to
blend until smooth.

HOW TO MAKE
Yoghurt

YOGHURT HAS SO MANY USES – IT MAKES AN EXCELLENT BASE FOR MARINADES, DIPS AND TOPPINGS AND IS OFTEN USED TO ADD RICHNESS AND A TANG TO SAUCES DURING COOKING. IF THIS IS YOUR FIRST TIME MAKING YOGHURT, START BY CHECKING IT AFTER 4 HOURS AND STOP WHEN IT REACHES A FLAVOUR AND CONSISTENCY YOU LIKE. AVOID STIRRING THE YOGHURT UNTIL IT HAS FULLY SET. THE EXACT TIME WILL DEPEND ON THE CULTURES USED, THE TEMPERATURE OF THE YOGHURT AND YOUR YOGHURT PREFERENCES – THE LONGER YOGHURT SITS, THE THICKER AND MORE TART IT BECOMES.

MAKES ABOUT 2KG YOGHURT | PREPARATION TIME: ABOUT 6 HOURS
COOKING TIME: 15 MINUTES | SETTING TIME: 4–8 HOURS

EQUIPMENT

HEAVY-BASED SAUCEPAN WITH A LID
SPATULA
THERMOMETER
SMALL MEASURING CUP OR BOWL
WHISK

93°C

Cool

Whisk

1

Preheat the oven to 160°C/315°F/Gas 2–3. Pour 2.3 litres full-cream (whole) milk into a heavy-based saucepan with a lid and heat over a medium–high heat. Warm the milk to just below boiling, about 93°C/200°F. Gently stir the milk, making sure the bottom doesn't scorch and the milk doesn't boil over.

Note For best results use organic full-cream milk.

2

Let the milk cool until it is warm to the touch, 44–46°C/110–115°F. Stir occasionally to prevent a skin from forming.

3

Scoop out about 250ml of warm milk and add it to 130g whole yoghurt (containing active cultures) in a bowl. Whisk until smooth and the yoghurt is dissolved into the milk.

4 hours

5

Cover the mixture with the lid and wrap the pan with tea towels. Place in the turned-off oven. Let the yoghurt set for at least 4 hours, or overnight.

Pour

4

While whisking the warm milk gently, pour the whisked yoghurt back into the milk pan. Switch off the oven at this point.

Yoghurt

6

Once the yoghurt has set to your liking, remove it from the oven. If you see any watery whey on the surface of the yoghurt, you can either drain this off or whisk it back into the yoghurt before transferring it to containers. Whisking also gives the yoghurt a more consistent creamy texture. Transfer into sterilised jars, seal with tight-fitting sterilised lids, and refrigerate for 2 weeks.

Cucumber, Carrot and Mint Chutney

THIS IS A CLASSIC YOGHURT CHUTNEY. THIS RECIPE HAS TAKEN THIS CHUTNEY ONE STEP FURTHER BY ADDING CARROT, WHICH GIVES IT AN EXTRA BITE. IT'S A COOLING ACCOMPANIMENT TO ANY FIERY CURRY.

SERVES 4 | PREPARATION TIME: 15 MINUTES

FRESH

115g carrot, grated

115g cucumber, grated and squeezed dry using a muslin (cheese cloth) or clean tea towel

¼ garlic clove, very finely chopped

225g Greek-style yoghurt

¼ small green chilli, seeded (optional) and finely chopped

SPICES

¼ teaspoon toasted cumin seeds, lightly crushed, reserving a pinch to garnish

black salt or salt, to taste

large pinch of chaat masala

PANTRY/LARDER

¼ teaspoon dried mint

OPTIONAL GARNISH

1 tablespoon finely chopped Spring Onion, Coriander and Mint (see page 232)

Place all the ingredients in a bowl and mix together. Garnish, if desired, and serve cold.

South Indian Eggplant Pickle

A POPULAR VEGETABLE IN INDIAN COOKING, EGGPLANT IS USED
IN MANY INNOVATIVE WAYS. THIS TANGY, SWEET PICKLE HAS
A FIERY KICK AND PARTNERS WELL WITH PANCAKES, RICE,
DHAL DISHES AND CRISPY CRACKERS.

MAKES 350ML | PREPARATION TIME: 2 HOURS | DRAINING TIME: 3 HOURS

FRESH

500g eggplant (aubergine), diced
into medium-sized cubes

55g piece ginger, peeled

4 garlic cloves

8–9 fresh curry leaves

3½ teaspoons tamarind pulp

SPICES

1 tablespoon black mustard seeds

3½ teaspoons fennel seeds

1 tablespoon cumin seeds

2½ teaspoons chilli powder

3 teaspoons ground turmeric

PANTRY/LARDER

1½ tablespoons salt

125ml pickling vinegar

120ml mustard seed oil
(see page 15) or oil

220g soft brown sugar

1. Place the eggplant in a large colander, coat and gently massage with the salt, then leave to drain for about 3 hours.

2. Take handfuls of eggplant and squeeze out the water until very dry.

3. Use a mortar and pestle or a small blender to grind the ginger, garlic and 1 tablespoon of the vinegar until a fine paste forms. Set aside.

4. Heat the oil in a large heavy-based frying pan over a medium heat. Fry the eggplant in 2 batches for about 3–4 minutes, or until soft and golden, removing each batch with a slotted spoon and setting aside.

5. Reduce the heat, and in the same pan, gently fry the mustard, fennel and cumin seeds and the curry leaves for 20 seconds.

6. Add the garlic and ginger paste and fry for 2–3 minutes, then add the chilli powder and turmeric and fry for 30 seconds.

7. Pour in the remaining vinegar, the tamarind pulp and sugar, stir through and cook for 1 minute, then add the eggplant and stir-fry for a further 12–15 minutes, or until the liquid has reduced and it has become sticky.

8. Remove the pan from the heat and cool completely. Place in a sterilised jar with a tight-fitting lid and chill for 5–6 weeks.

Fruit Chutney

THIS CHUTNEY IS SOFT, GOOEY AND EDGY, SO IT'S WELL SUITED
TO HOT CURRIES AND BREADS, BUT CHEEKILY SITS WELL IN CHEESE
SANDWICHES OR AS PART OF A CHEESE BOARD.

SERVES 4 | PREPARATION TIME: 30 MINUTES | COOKING TIME: 20 MINUTES

FRESH
1 garlic clove, crushed
½ teaspoon grated ginger
3 tablespoons tamarind pulp
60g finely chopped pears
60g finely chopped apples

SPICES
½ teaspoon ground turmeric
2 teaspoons chilli powder
1 teaspoon toasted cumin seeds
½ teaspoon black salt or chaat masala

PANTRY/LARDER
55g dried pitted dates, finely chopped
180g raisins
180ml cider vinegar
3 tablespoons soft brown sugar
salt, to taste

1. Place all the ingredients and 4 tablespoons water, in a heavy-based saucepan over a low–medium heat and stir constantly until the sugar has dissolved.

2. Reduce the heat to low and simmer gently, stirring frequently for about 20 minutes, periodically checking if any extra water is needed, or until the fruit is soft.

3. Remove the pan from the heat and cool completely. Place in a sterilised jar with a tight-fitting lid and refrigerate for 5–6 weeks.

Apple Pickle

MAKE THIS PICKLE IN ADVANCE, AS THE SPICES NEED TO INFUSE
AND SETTLE. THE TOASTED SPICES MAKE A REAL DIFFERENCE
TO THIS TART APPLE CONDIMENT. EAT ALONGSIDE CHEESE,
BREADS AND PLAIN PARANTHA (SEE PAGE 120).

SERVES 4–6 | PREPARATION TIME: 30 MINUTES | STANDING TIME: 1½ HOURS

FRESH

260g sour cooking apples,
cored and thinly sliced

1 red chilli, slit lengthways
down the middle

7–8 fresh curry leaves

6–8 whole garlic cloves

SPICES

1 teaspoon fennel seeds

2 teaspoons mustard seeds

1 tablespoon chilli powder

½ teaspoon ground turmeric

½ teaspoon fenugreek seeds

PANTRY/LARDER

3 teaspoons soft brown sugar

2 teaspoons salt, or to taste

2–3 tablespoons oil

4 tablespoons white wine vinegar

1. Heat a non-stick frying pan over a low heat. Add the fennel and mustard seeds and toast and toss for about 40–60 seconds. Cool and grind to a powder using a mortar and pestle. Set aside.

2. In a large bowl, mix together the apples, chilli powder, turmeric, sugar and salt to taste, making sure the apples are well coated. Leave to stand for 10 minutes.

3. Heat the oil in a heavy-based frying pan or wok over a low–medium heat. Add the red chilli, garlic, curry leaves and fenugreek seeds and fry gently for 30–40 seconds.

4. Stir in the mustard and fennel powder and keep mixing and frying for 1 minute.

5. Stir in the apples and vinegar, making sure they are all well coated, and cook for a further 5 minutes.

6. Remove the pan from the heat, cover with a lid and leave to rest for 1–1½ hours. Once cooled completely, transfer to a sterilised jar with a tight-fitting lid and refrigerate for 3–5 weeks.

NOTE: Give the apples a good rub with a clean tea towel before adding them to the pan, as there should be no moisture.

Garlic, Ginger and Red Chilli Pickle

THREE BOLD INGREDIENTS THAT COME TOGETHER AND HAVE AN IMPACT ON ANY DHAL, PARANTHA OR VEGETABLE DISH. THE LONGER IT STEWS IN SPICES THE MORE TENDER AND SWEET THIS PICKLE BECOMES.

SERVES 4 | PREPARATION TIME: 15 MINUTES | COOKING TIME: 15–18 MINUTES

FRESH

50g garlic cloves, cut into thick slices

50g piece ginger, peeled and cut into julienne

2–4 red bird's eye chillies

SPICES

¾ teaspoon fenugreek seeds

½ teaspoon ground turmeric

¼ teaspoon chilli powder

PANTRY/LARDER

1½ tablespoons oil

150ml pickling vinegar

1 teaspoon soft brown sugar

¼ teaspoon salt, or to taste

1. Heat the oil in a frying pan over a low–medium heat.

2. Add the fenugreek seeds and fry for 20 seconds, then add the garlic followed by the ginger and stir-fry for 4–5 minutes.

3. Add the turmeric, chilli powder, vinegar, whole chillies, sugar and salt. Reduce the heat and cook, stirring, for 10–12 minutes, or until the liquid has evaporated and the garlic is tender. Use at once or transfer to a sterilised jar with a tight-fitting lid and store in the refrigerator for 1–2 weeks.

Sticky, Hot Mango and Lime Pickle

EVERYTHING A PICKLE SHOULD BE – STICKY, HOT AND ESSENTIAL.
A RESTAURANT FAVOURITE, IT HAS BEEN EATEN IN ABUNDANCE
WITH POPPADOMS AND FRIED SNACKS.

MAKES ABOUT 175G | PREPARATION TIME: 10 MINUTES
STANDING TIME: 15 MINUTES | COOKING TIME: 10–15 MINUTES

FRESH

4 mangoes, peeled and cut
into medium-sized cubes

grated zest and juice of 1 lime

SPICES

2 tablespoons chilli powder

2 teaspoons panch phoran (see page 13)

PANTRY/LARDER

1½ teaspoons salt

175g soft brown sugar

2 tablespoons oil

1. In a bowl, toss the mangoes with the salt and chilli powder. Leave to stand for 15 minutes.

2. Heat the oil in a large frying pan or wok over a low–medium heat. Add the panch phoran and stir-fry for 25 seconds.

3. Next, add the chilli-coated mango cubes, toss and cook for 6–8 minutes, then add the lime zest and juice. Cover with a lid and cook for 5–7 minutes.

4. Add the sugar and cook, uncovered, until any liquid has evaporated and the mangoes are tender and not mushy.

5. Remove the pan from the heat and cool. Place in a sterilised jar with a tight-fitting lid and refrigerate for up to 2–3 weeks.

Preserved Lemons, Peppercorns with Ginger and Garlic

GIVEN TIME THIS HEALTHY AYURVEDIC PICKLE JUST KEEPS ON GETTING BETTER, AS THE RIND BECOMES MORE TENDER AND ROBUST. FINELY CHOP THIS PICKLE AND USE IN SALADS, OR AS PART OF MARINADES, DRESSINGS AND GARNISHES. OTHERWISE EAT JUST SIMPLY AS AN ACCOMPANIMENT TO MAIN MEALS AND SNACKS.

MAKES ABOUT 200G | PREPARATION TIME: 15 MINUTES

FRESH
6–7 unwaxed lemons, halved then each half cut into 3 wedges

8–10 garlic cloves

60g piece ginger, peeled and cut into long slivers

30g whole stem fresh peppercorns

SPICES
1 teaspoon ground turmeric

3 teaspoons chilli powder (optional)

PANTRY/LARDER
about 200g sea salt flakes

2 teaspoons soft brown sugar

NOTE
If not using unwaxed lemons, make sure to scrub them really well before use.

Make sure the garlic and ginger are super-dry.

1. Place the lemons, garlic, ginger and peppercorns in a large bowl and cover with the turmeric, chilli powder, if using, salt and sugar.

2. Using your hands, rub in the spices, making sure everything is well coated.

3. Transfer the mixture to a sterilised jar with a tight-fitting lid.

4. Place the jar in direct sunlight for 6–8 days, making sure to shake vigorously every other day. Refrigerate for 4–6 weeks.

SIX
Yoghurts

❶ ROAST EGGPLANT

PREHEAT the grill to a medium setting.

RUB oil over 1 large eggplant (aubergine), prick all over and grill for 20 minutes. Turn every 3–4 minutes until the skin is scorched and the flesh is soft.

LEAVE the eggplant to cool, then remove the skin and finely chop or mash the flesh.

HEAT 1½ teaspoons oil in a frying pan. Add ¼ teaspoon cumin seeds, 4–5 fresh curry leaves, ¼ teaspoon ginger, ¼ finely chopped onion and fry over a low heat, stirring, for 1–2 minutes. Stir in ¼ teaspoon ground coriander, ¼ teaspoon chilli powder and season with salt. Fry for 30 seconds.

STIR in the eggplant and cook for 6–8 minutes.

REMOVE from the heat, cool, then place in a bowl and mix in 340g natural or Greek-style yoghurt.

GARNISH with finely chopped coriander and 1½ teaspoons pomegranate seeds, if liked.

❷ POTATO AND TOASTED CUMIN

BOIL 1 large potato with skin on, then cool and chop into small cubes.

DRY-ROAST the following whole spices: 1 teaspoon cumin seeds, 1 teaspoon pomegranate seeds and ¼ teaspoon coriander seeds in a non-stick frying pan.

COOL then, use a mortar and pestle to grind until coarse. Reserve 1 teaspoon for the garnish.

MIX the rest with the potatoes, 340g natural yoghurt and ¼ teaspoon chaat masala.

SEASON with sea salt and coarse black pepper.

GARNISH with a sprinkling of reserved spice mix and finely chopped coriander.

❸ SPINACH AND MINT

PUT 5–6 mint leaves, a large pinch of dried mint, 1 finely chopped garlic clove, 1 teaspoon toasted cumin seeds and a large pinch of salt in a mortar.

GRIND with the pestle to make a smooth paste.

PLACE 225g cooked chopped spinach into a bowl, together with the mint paste and stir in 225g natural or Greek-style yoghurt.

GARNISH with 2cm piece peeled and grated ginger and fine slivers of red chilli, if liked.

❹ CRISPY OKRA

PLACE 225g natural or Greek-style yoghurt in a bowl.

STIR in ¼ teaspoon dried mint, a large pinch of chilli powder, ¼ teaspoon chaat masala and salt to taste.

GARNISH with 2 tablespoons Crispy Okra (see page 232) and a large pinch of toasted and finely crushed cumin seeds and toasted sesame seeds, if liked.

❺ RAW VEGETABLES

MIX together ½ very finely chopped small carrot, ¼ celery stick, ¼ green capsicum (pepper), ¼ red onion, 1 tablespoon finely chopped coriander and 1 small seeded tomato in a large bowl.

STIR in 225g natural or Greek-style yoghurt, 1 finely crushed garlic clove, ¼ teaspoon ground cumin and salt to taste.

HEAT ¼ tablespoon oil in a frying pan and fry ½ teaspoon black mustard seeds, ½ thinly sliced red chilli and 3–4 fresh curry leaves.

COOL slightly and stir into the yoghurt, reserving a little for the garnish.

❻ CARROT, CUCUMBER AND CORIANDER

MIX together in a large bowl, grated or tiny cubes ½ small carrot, 5cm piece cucumber, seeded, grated or chopped into tiny cubes (squeezed dry using muslin or a clean tea towel), ¼ very finely chopped garlic clove, ¼ finely chopped small green chilli (seeded, optional), ¼ teaspoon dried mint, ¼ teaspoon ground cumin, a large pinch of chaat masala (optional), 225g natural yoghurt, salt and coarse black pepper to taste.

GARNISH with 1 tablespoon finely chopped Spring Onion, Coriander and Mint (see page 232), if liked.

Desserts and Drinks

CHAPTER 7

Pistachio Kulfi

THIS IS A QUICK VERSION OF A CLASSIC INDIAN ICE CREAM.
ALTERNATIVELY, REPLACE OR MIX THE PISTACHIOS WITH FINELY CHOPPED
DRIED OR FRESH FRUIT AND OR MIXED NUTS. IT IS DELICIOUS ON ITS
OWN OR SERVE WITH GRIDDLED OR BARBECUED TROPICAL FRUIT.

SERVES 4 | PREPARATION TIME: 10 MINUTES | FREEZING TIME: AT LEAST 6 HOURS

FRESH
600ml double or whipping cream

SPICES
2 pinches of saffron threads,
soaked in a little warm milk
2 pinches of green cardamom seeds
1 teaspoon kewra water (optional)

PANTRY/LARDER
600ml condensed milk
600ml evaporated milk
2 tablespoons pistachios,
finely chopped

1. In a large bowl, thoroughly mix together the cream, condensed milk and evaporated milk.

2. Add the soaked saffron with its soaking water, cardamom seeds and kewra water, if using, to the milk mixture and combine.

3. Finally, add most of the chopped pistachios, setting a spoonful aside for the decoration, and stir until the mixture is well combined. Pour the mixture into a freezer-proof container.

4. Freeze for at least 6 hours. Remove 5–10 minutes before serving and decorate with the reserved pistachios.

NOTE: Stir the ice cream once halfway through, so the nuts don't settle at the bottom.

It can also be frozen in individual moulds.

Almond and Saffron Cake

A SUPER-MOIST AND FEATHERLIGHT CAKE, IT HAS
BITTER HINTS OF ORANGE PEEL AND GENTLE POPS OF CARDAMOM.
SERVE AND ENJOY ANY TIME OF THE DAY.

SERVES 8–10 | PREPARATION TIME: 1 HOUR | COOKING TIME: 50–55 MINUTES

FRESH

2 unwaxed oranges (about 280g
including skin), roughly chopped

5 eggs, separated

SPICES

small pinch of ground
cardamom seeds

pinch of saffron threads,
soaked in warm milk

PANTRY/LARDER

200g caster sugar

225g ground almonds

2 tablespoons flaked almonds

2 tablespoons sifted icing sugar

1. Preheat the oven to 180°C/350°F/Gas 4, then line the base and side of a 23cm springform cake tin with baking paper.

2. Place the oranges in a saucepan with 1 tablespoon water. Cover with a lid and cook gently for 30 minutes, or until soft and the liquid has evaporated. Remove the pan from the heat and cool, then place the oranges in a blender and finely chop. Alternatively, use a knife.

3. Whisk the egg whites in a clean, dry bowl until they form soft peaks. Gradually stir in half the caster sugar and continue to whisk for 1 minute.

4. Next, in a separate bowl, whisk the egg yolks together with the remaining caster sugar for 2–3 minutes. Whisk in the oranges, then gently fold the ground almonds, cardamom seeds and saffron into the milk. Using a large metal spoon, slowly fold in spoonfuls of the egg whites until everything is well combined.

5. Pour the mixture into the prepared tin, sprinkle the flaked almonds over the top and bake in the oven for 50–55 minutes, checking every 20 minutes or until golden brown.

6. Leave the cake to cool in the tin before turning out and dusting with icing sugar. Store the cake in an airtight container for 2–3 days.

Carrot and Orange Balls with Chocolate

THIS IS AN IMPRESSIVE DESSERT, ESPECIALLY IF PILED HIGH LIKE
A PYRAMID, DRIZZLED WITH RIPPLES OF HOT DARK CHOCOLATE
AND A SCATTERING OF TOASTED MIXED NUTS, OR SERVE THE HOT
CHOCOLATE ON THE SIDE AS A DIP.

SERVES 4–6 | PREPARATION TIME: 30 MINUTES | COOKING TIME: 1½ HOURS

FRESH

450g carrots, finely grated

grated zest of 1 large
unwaxed orange

720ml full-cream (whole) milk

SPICES

6–8 green cardamom pods

PANTRY/LARDER

55g very finely chopped almonds

140g caster sugar

85g ghee or unsalted butter

2 tablespoons pistachios

1 bar (150g) good-quality
dark chocolate

2 tablespoons flaked almonds,
lightly toasted

1. Put the carrots, orange zest, chopped almonds, sugar and milk into a heavy-based saucepan and stir over a low heat until the sugar has dissolved. Cook over a medium heat for about 1½ hours. The pan should be stirred from time to time to prevent the carrots from sticking to the bottom. Cook until the mixture thickens and most of the liquid has evaporated. Keep stirring, especially during the latter stage of cooking.

2. Using a mortar and pestle or a rolling pin, gently break the cardamom pods and crush the seeds.

3. Melt the ghee or butter in a separate saucepan and add the crushed cardamom pods and seeds. Stir in the carrot mixture and fry over a low–medium heat until the carrot mixture becomes reddish brown.

4. Remove the pan from the heat and cool. Once the mixture has cooled, pick out the cardamom pods. Take a dessertspoonful of mixture and roll into a smooth ball. Continue until the mixture is finished. Lay the balls on a flat platter or pile high, creating a tall pyramid.

5. Toast the pistachios in a dry frying pan over a low heat until light golden brown. Remove from the heat and cool.

6. Break the chocolate into pieces and put into a heatproof bowl. Place the bowl over a saucepan of gently simmering water, making sure the bowl does not touch the water and leave to melt.

7. Using a rolling pin, roughly crush the toasted, flaked almonds and pistachios.

8. Liberally drizzle the balls with hot melted chocolate and shower with the toasted flaked almonds and pistachios.

NOTE: It is important that the pan is heavy-based, otherwise there is a risk of the pan and carrot mix burning.

Whole Spiced Fruit Salad

A SIMPLE AND LIGHT DESSERT, WHICH WOULD BE PERFECT
OFFERED AT THE END OF A RICH MEAL. SERVE ALONGSIDE GOOD-QUALITY
ICE CREAM OR ADD A DROP OF RUM AND GINGER PEELINGS
TO THE SUGAR SYRUP.

SERVES 4–5 | PREPARATION TIME: 40 MINUTES
STANDING TIME: 1 HOUR | COOKING TIME: 6–7 MINUTES

FRESH

grated zest and juice of 1 lime

grated zest and juice of 1 lemon

1 small pineapple

1 large mango, thinly sliced
or chopped

2 kiwi fruit, thinly sliced

1 large blood orange, peeled
and cut into segments

5 lychees, halved

½ papaya, thinly sliced

2 passionfruit

4 tablespoons blueberries

SPICES

2 cloves

1 star anise

1 cinnamon stick

1 vanilla pod, split open lengthways
and seeds scraped out

PANTRY/LARDER

110g caster sugar

1. Mix together the sugar, 110ml water, cloves, star anise, cinnamon stick, vanilla pod and seeds in a saucepan. Simmer gently until the sugar has dissolved, then continue simmering for a further 5–6 minutes.

2. Stir in the lime and lemon zest and juice, then remove the pan from the heat and leave to cool completely.

3. Meanwhile, put all the fruit into a serving dish, then pour or strain the sugar syrup over the fruit. Leave to stand for at least 1 hour before serving.

Pomegranate, Lime and Rosewater Granita

THIS SEMI-FROZEN DESSERT IS SO SIMPLE AND WORKS WELL WITH MOST FLAVOURS – FOR EXAMPLE, TRY WATERMELON, PINEAPPLE, BLOOD ORANGE, LEMON AND MINT, OR BLUEBERRY. ALTERNATIVELY, ENJOY AS A DRINK – JUST SCOOP A LARGE SPOONFUL INTO A BEAUTIFUL GLASS, ADD A TEASPOON OF POMEGRANATE SEEDS AND TOP UP WITH CHILLED PROSECCO.

SERVES 4 | PREPARATION TIME: 20 MINUTES | FREEZING TIME: 2½ HOURS

FRESH
400ml pomegranate juice
125ml orange juice
juice of ½ lime

SPICES
1 teaspoon rosewater

PANTRY/LARDER
50g golden caster sugar

1. Place the orange and pomegranate juices and the sugar in a saucepan and stir over a low heat until the sugar has dissolved. Combine with the lime juice and rosewater and set aside to cool.

2. Pour the mixture into a flat metal container. Carefully place in the freezer and freeze until solid, about 2 hours, then whisk with a fork and return to the freezer for a further 1–2 hours.

3. Scoop and serve immediately.

NOTE: It's important to freeze the granita in a metal tray because the metal keeps the mixture colder and at the right consistency.

Stir to break up the ice crystals at 1-hour intervals until the granita is light and easy to scoop.

Creamy Honey and Raisin Vermicelli Pots

THIS IS A RICH AND COMFORTING DESSERT, WHICH CAN BE
EATEN HOT OR COLD AND ONLY TAKES MINUTES TO MAKE. ENRICH
THIS DISH EVEN FURTHER BY SERVING WITH ROASTED OR
STEWED PLUMS, APPLES OR PEACHES.

SERVES 4 | PREPARATION TIME: 10 MINUTES | COOKING TIME: 8–10 MINUTES

FRESH

500ml full-cream (whole) milk

grated zest of 1 unwaxed orange

1 tablespoon double cream

SPICES

¼ teaspoon ground cardamom seeds

PANTRY/LARDER

2 tablespoons ghee or unsalted butter

100–125g fine wheat vermicelli,
broken into small and
medium-sized pieces

3–4 tablespoons caster sugar

1 tablespoon raisins or finely
chopped apricots or dates

DECORATION

1 tablespoon runny honey

1 tablespoon flaked almonds,
lightly toasted

NOTE

Wheat vermicelli can also be
replaced with rice vermicelli.

1. Heat the ghee or butter in a heavy-based saucepan over a low–medium heat.

2. Add the broken vermicelli and stir-fry for about 1 minute, or until golden.

3. Reduce the heat and pour in the milk, sugar, ground cardamom seeds, raisins and orange zest. Stir and gently simmer for 5 minutes, then add the cream and continue cooking for a further 2–3 minutes, or until it thickens.

4. Turn off the heat, serve in individual pots and decorate with honey and flaked almonds.

Masala Chai

TO GIVE THIS BLEND AN EXTRA INDULGENT TOUCH ADD DRIED ROSE
PETALS AND SAFFRON, OR FOR A MORE EARTHY FLAVOUR TRY
NUTMEG AND STAR ANISE. FOR A FASTER, AND LIGHTER TEA, TAKE A
TEASPOON OF THIS BLEND AND INFUSE IN A POT OF TEA, THEN MAKE
IT THE TRADITIONAL WAY WITH A DROP OF COLD MILK.

MAKES 1 CUP | PREPARATION TIME: 15 MINUTES | COOKING TIME: 8–10 MINUTES

SPICES

85g fennel seeds

30 green cardamom pods,
slightly cracked

1½ teaspoons cloves

1½ cinnamon sticks

3 teaspoons ground ginger

55g mace

PANTRY/LARDER

sugar, to taste

1. Heat a frying pan over a low heat and dry-roast the fennel seeds, cardamom pods, cloves and cinnamon sticks for 5–7 minutes. Remove from the heat and allow to cool completely.

2. Place the roasted spices together with the remaining spices in a mortar and using a pestle and grind to a very coarse powder. Store in an airtight container for up to 2 months.

3. For 1 cup of chai, boil the milk, 100ml water, 2 teaspoons masala and 1 teabag in a saucepan over a medium heat for 4–5 minutes. Gradually bring to the boil, then reduce the heat and add sugar, to taste. Strain and serve.

NOTE: Masala chai and hot samosas make the perfect and most irresistible partnership.

Ayurvedic Jamu Tonic Drink

THIS IS A HIGHLY ANTIOXIDANT AYURVEDIC TONIC THAT CAN ALSO HELP TO IMPROVE BLOOD CIRCULATION. FOR MAXIMUM BENEFITS, DRINK WARM OR COLD EVERY DAY, THROUGHOUT THE DAY.

MAKES 1 LITRE | PREPARATION TIME: 1 HOUR

FRESH

juice of 2 limes

SPICES

40g ground turmeric or 1½ teaspoons peeled, finely grated fresh root if available

PANTRY/LARDER

1 tablespoon agave syrup (natural sweetener) (optional)

75g dry tamarind

5 tablespoons manuka honey

1. Place 1 litre filtered water, the turmeric, agave and tamarind together in a saucepan. Bring to the boil and boil for 30 minutes.

2. Remove from the heat, add the lime juice and manuka honey. Stir well and leave to cool for as long as possible.

3. Once cool, strain into a jug with a lid. It can be stored in the refrigerator for up to 2 days.

Chilli Hot Chocolate

THIS QUIRKY, CHILLI-SPIKED HOT CHOCOLATE DRINK IS SPICED UP
WITH RED CHILLI FLAKES AND BACKED UP WITH A WARM SWEETNESS,
WHICH COMES FROM THE NUTMEG AND CINNAMON. SERVE WITH
SWEET FRUIT BREAD – PERFECT FOR DIPPING.

SERVES 4 | PREPARATION TIME: 5 MINUTES
STANDING TIME: 8–10 MINUTES | COOKING TIME: 15 MINUTES

FRESH

750ml full-cream (whole) milk
75ml light (single) cream

SPICES

1 cinnamon stick
pinch of grated nutmeg
1 dried red chilli

PANTRY/LARDER

25g drinking chocolate powder
150g good-quality dark chocolate,
at least 70% cocoa solids,
roughly chopped
sugar (optional)

DECORATION

small pinch of red chilli flakes

SERVE

6 tablespoons whipped
double cream
grated chocolate

1. Heat the milk, cream, cinnamon stick, nutmeg and dried chilli in a heavy-based saucepan over a medium–high heat. Bring to the boil, then remove from the heat and set aside for 8–10 minutes to infuse.

2. Strain into a clean pan and reheat over a low heat for 2–3 minutes (don't boil).

3. Reduce the heat, add the chocolate powder and chopped chocolate and whisk until smooth and melted.

4. Serve with whipped cream, grated chocolate and a very small sprinkle of chilli flakes, adding sugar, if liked.

Cardamom Coffee

A GOOD-QUALITY COFFEE THAT'S SERVED WITH SMOKY AND EARTHY
CARDAMOM MILK, ENJOY THIS COFFEE AS AN EARLY MORNING DRINK
OR POUR INTO SHOT GLASSES AND SERVE AT THE END OF A
DELICIOUS MEAL. YOU CAN ALSO REPLACE WITH ANY SPICES YOU
DESIRE – CINNAMON, NUTMEG OR STAR ANISE.

MAKES 2 CUPS | PREPARATION TIME: 5 MINUTES | COOKING TIME: 5–6 MINUTES

FRESH
150ml milk

SPICES
5–6 cardamom pods, slightly cracked

PANTRY/LARDER
80ml freshly brewed coffee of your choice
sugar, to taste

1. In a saucepan, heat the milk and cardamom pods over a low–medium heat for 4–5 minutes, stirring and whisking frequently to create a froth. Leave to stand and infuse.

2. Strain and gently heat when ready to use.

3. Pour your already made hot coffee into pots or cups, add sugar and pour in the spiced milk through a strainer.

Ayurvedic Detox Tea

THIS SIMPLE CLEANSING TEA HELPS TO NOURISH YOUR BODY, METABOLISM AND DIGESTIVE SYSTEM. TRY TO DRINK THIS SPICE-INFUSED WATER THROUGHOUT THE DAY. ADD A LITTLE HONEY OR APPLE JUICE FOR A BIT OF SWEETNESS.

MAKES 1 LITRE | PREPARATION TIME: 5 MINUTES
STANDING TIME: 10–15 MINUTES | COOKING TIME: 10 MINUTES

FRESH
2 thin slices of ginger

SPICES
1 teaspoon cumin seeds
5 cloves
½ teaspoon black peppercorns
1 teaspoon fennel seeds
1 teaspoon coriander seeds
1 cinnamon stick

1. Pour 1 litre filtered water into a large saucepan, add the ginger and all the spices and bring to the boil, then reduce the heat and simmer for 5–10 minutes.

2. Turn off the heat. Cover with a lid and leave to infuse for about 10–15 minutes. Drink hot or cold.

Fresh Lemon and Lime Soda

SOUR, SWEET AND SALTY COMBINATION DRINKS WORK WELL
ALONGSIDE HOT FIERY DISHES, BUT THEY ARE EQUALLY COOLING AS A
STAND-ALONE DRINK – ADD A SPLASH OF GIN FOR A FURTHER TWIST.

SERVES 6 | PREPARATION TIME: ABOUT 15 MINUTES | STANDING TIME: 10 MINUTES

FRESH
125ml lime juice (about 6–7 limes)
125ml lemon juice (about 6–7 lemons)
½ lime, cut into slices
½ lemon, cut into slices

PANTRY/LARDER
½ teaspoon salt
2 tablespoons caster sugar
1 litre soda, tonic or sparkling water

SERVE
ice cubes

1. In a small jug, mix together the lime juice, lemon juice, salt and sugar. Leave to stand for 10 minutes, or until the sugar and salt have dissolved. Reserve until ready to serve.

2. Pour a little into each glass, add the lime and lemon slices, then top up with soda, tonic or sparkling water. Serve with ice cubes.

Sweet and Salted Lassi

LASSI IS A LIGHT AND TRADITIONAL YOGHURT-BASED DRINK. IN INDIA, THIS COOLING BLEND OF YOGHURT, WATER, SPICES AND SOMETIMES FRUIT IS A POPULAR BEVERAGE TO HAVE ON SUPER-HOT DAYS OR AS AN ACCOMPANIMENT TO SPICY DISHES. LASSI CAN ALSO BE REFRIGERATED FOR A COUPLE OF HOURS BEFORE SERVING.

MAKES 2–3 GLASSES | PREPARATION TIME: 5–10 MINUTES

SALTED

FRESH
600g chilled natural yoghurt

SPICES
1½ teaspoons toasted cumin seeds, coarsely crushed

1 teaspoon black salt or salt

PANTRY/LARDER
7–8 ice cubes, crushed

DECORATION
5–6 mint leaves, finely shredded

1. In a jug, whisk together the yoghurt, 250ml chilled water, cumin (reserving a little for the decoration) and salt and mix together until smooth and frothy.

2. Pour into a tall glass and decorate with mint and the reserved cumin.

SWEET

FRESH
350g natural yoghurt

125ml water or cold milk

SPICES
large pinch of ground cardamom

small pinch of saffron threads, soaked in a little warm water

1 teaspoon rosewater

PANTRY/LARDER
2 tablespoons sugar

7–8 crushed ice cubes

DECORATION
1 tablespoon mixed crushed pistachios and blanched almonds

1. In a jug, whisk together the yoghurt, ground cardamom (reserving a little for the decoration), saffron, rosewater, sugar and water or milk until smooth and frothy.

2. Pour into glasses and decorate with crushed nuts and the reserved ground cardamom.

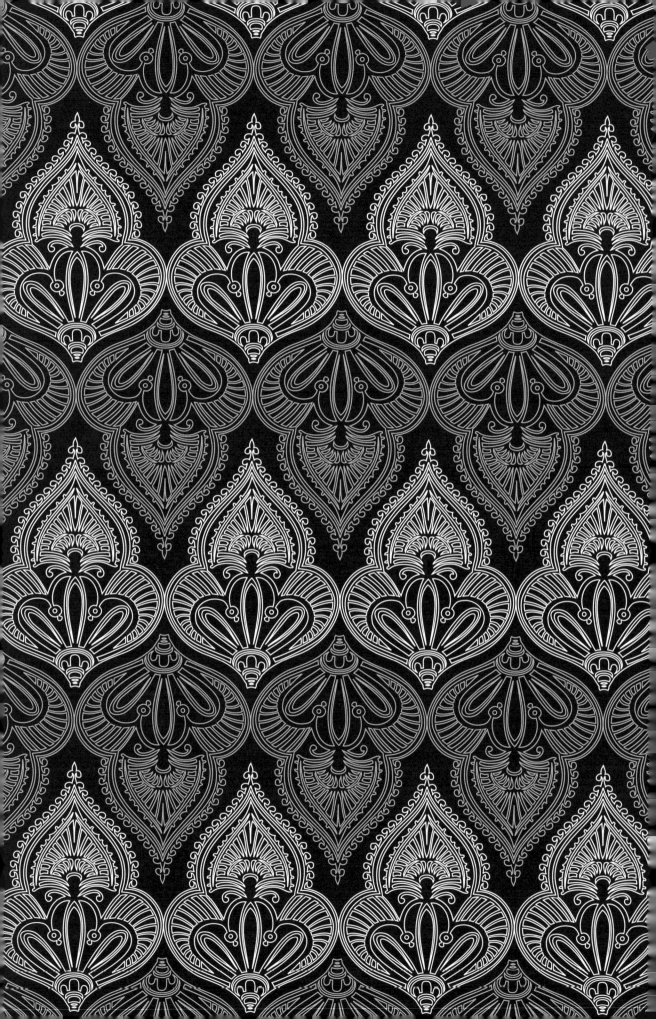

Basics

CHAPTER 8

TAMARIND PULP

In most North Indian dishes tomatoes form the main base, but for South Indian dishes tamarind is the key ingredient, especially for sauce-based dishes. This tart, fruit pulp is used to add tang and sourness. It is very versatile and easy to prepare, so make a large amount and use in marinades, dips, chutneys or rice, vegetable and fish dishes.

MAKES ABOUT 350–500G
PREPARATION TIME: ABOUT 10 MINUTES
COOKING TIME: ABOUT 10–12 MINUTES

FRESH
200g block of seedless tamarind

1. Place the tamarind and 350ml water together in a saucepan and simmer gently for 10–12 minutes until softened through. Drain through a fine sieve, using the back of a spoon to keep scraping it until you are left with seed and fibres. If it's cool enough use your hands to further loosen the pulp.

2. Pour the tamarind pulp into a screw-top jar and refrigerate. Use within 1 month.

SAFFRON ESSENCE

Saffron is a high-quality spice, and is the most expensive in the world. A tiny amount of these delicate threads do go a long way. Presoaking your saffron draws out the colour and helps to ensure the flavours infuse evenly throughout the dish.

MAKES ABOUT 55ML
PREPARATION TIME: ABOUT 10 MINUTES
SOAKING TIME: 15–25 MINUTES

SPICES
2–3 saffron threads

PANTRY/LARDER
50ml warm cooking liquid, such as milk, water or stock

1. Immerse the saffron threads in the hot liquid and soak for about 15–25 minutes.

2. Pour the liquid together with the saffron into your dish – usually towards the end of your cooking.

ESSENTIAL PASTES

THE USE OF THESE TWO PASTES IS PARAMOUNT IN INDIAN
COOKING, SO IT'S WORTH MAKING THEM IN LARGE BATCHES,
OR PREP THE PASTES 2 DAYS BEFORE ENTERTAINING,
SO ALL THE GROUNDWORK HAS BEEN DONE.

CARAMELISED ONION PASTE

A sweet, silky smooth paste for all onion-based sauces or even marinades, it gives any dish a glossy sleek finish. To make a richer paste, blend with cashews, yoghurt or fried garlic and ginger.

MAKES 450G
PREPARATION TIME: ABOUT 10 MINUTES
COOKING TIME: ABOUT 30 MINUTES

FRESH
550g onions, thinly sliced

PANTRY/LARDER
4–5 tablespoons oil

1. Heat the oil in a heavy-based frying pan over a low–medium heat. Add the onions and fry, stirring, for 5–8 minutes.

2. Turn up the heat slightly, and keep stirring and frying for 15–20 minutes, or until the onions have become rich and golden.

3. Place the caramelised onions in a blender and blitz until smooth.

4. Place the paste in a jar and seal with a tight-fitting lid. Refrigerate for 1 week or place in small containers and freeze.

NOTE: Use a touch of water or extra oil if needed.

GINGER AND GARLIC PASTE

A fabulous paste that has endless uses. Use in all curries, marinades, dressing and dips. Prior to blending the ginger and garlic, you can also add a couple of fresh chillies.

MAKES 110G
PREPARATION TIME: ABOUT 10–12 MINUTES

FRESH
60g piece ginger, peeled and roughly chopped
80g garlic cloves, roughly chopped

1. Place the ginger and garlic together in a blender or use a mortar and pestle, and grind to a fine paste.

2. Place the paste in a jar and seal with a tight-fitting lid. Refrigerate for 3 days or place in small containers and freeze.

NOTE: Top with a little oil if storing for longer than 1–2 days.

SPRING ONION, CORIANDER AND MINT

This is refreshing and cleansing. Use to garnish yoghurt dishes, meats, chutneys and salads.

MAKES ABOUT 3 TABLESPOONS
PREPARATION TIME: ABOUT 5 MINUTES

FRESH
3 spring onions
¼ bunch coriander, including stalks
6–7 mint leaves

1. Very finely shred each ingredient, mix together and use immediately.

NOTE: Mint and coriander go black if left to stand for too long – if not using straight away, lightly coat the whole garnish with 1 teaspoon of oil and keep in the refrigerator.

CRISPY OKRA

This certainly is a different and interesting way to cook and eat okra. Use to garnish dhals, yoghurts, salads and rice or simply eat as a hot, crispy snack – if so, sprinkle, with a pinch of chaat masala while hot.

MAKES 500G
PREPARATION TIME: ABOUT 30 MINUTES
COOKING TIME: ABOUT 3–5 MINUTES

FRESH
500g okra, thinly sliced lengthways
¼ teaspoon lemon juice

SPICES
½ teaspoon garam masala
¼ teaspoon ground turmeric
1 teaspoon chilli powder

PANTRY/LARDER
1 tablespoon cornflour
¼ teaspoon salt
oil, for deep-frying

1. Wash and super-dry the okra. Cut lengthways down the middle, then cut into batons.

2. Place the okra in a bowl and sprinkle with all the lemon juice, spices, cornflour and salt.

3. Stir and coat evenly, then leave to absorb for about 20–25 minutes.

4. Heat the oil for deep-frying in a large, deep saucepan or a wok and deep-fry the okra in batches until golden and crisp. Remove and drain on paper towel. Cool completely.

HOW TO MAKE
Ghee

GHEE IS A TYPE OF CLARIFIED BUTTER, SIMMERED SLOWLY UNTIL
ALL THE MOISTURE EVAPORATES AND THE MILK SOLIDS BEGIN TO BROWN.
AS IT IS HEATED FOR LONGER, GHEE HAS A STRONG, NUTTY AND
CARAMEL-LIKE FLAVOUR AND AROMA. AYURVEDIC DEVOTEES CALL
GHEE LIQUID GOLD, AS IT HAS MANY HEALTH BENEFITS. IT IS ALSO
LACTOSE FRIENDLY AND HAS A HIGH BURNING POINT, SO IT'S
PERFECT FOR FRYING. IF YOU PREFER NOT TO COOK WITH GHEE,
THEN A FEW TEASPOONS DRIZZLED ON THE FINISHED DISH BEFORE
SERVING WILL GIVE IT THAT EXTRA EDGE OF FLAVOUR.

MAKES ABOUT 360ML | PREPARATION TIME: 5 MINUTES | COOKING TIME: 20–25 MINUTES

EQUIPMENT

HEAVY-BASED SAUCEPAN
FINE SIEVE
SEVERAL PIECES OF MUSLIN
MEASURING JUG
WOODEN SPOON

Cut

1

Place 450g good-quality
butter, cut into small cubes,
into a heavy-based saucepan.

Note For best results use
organic butter.

Melt

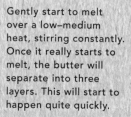

2

Gently start to melt
over a low–medium
heat, stirring constantly.
Once it really starts to
melt, the butter will
separate into three
layers. This will start to
happen quite quickly.

Check

3

Foam will appear on top,
milk solids will drop to the
bottom, and you should
be left with clarified
butter floating in between
the two. To check, use a
spoon to push back the
foam and take a look.

Simmer

Strain

5

Next, place a piece of muslin (cheesecloth) over a sterilised glass jar and carefully strain to remove the brown toasted milk proteins sitting at the base of the pan. Keep chilled for 6 months.

4

Bring the butter to a gentle simmer, turn down the heat and cook gently for a further 15–20 minutes, or until the middle layer becomes more fragrant and golden than when you first started. Push back the foam to take a look. With a fine sieve or a spoon, skim and lift off absolutely all the foam sitting on top and discard. All that should be left is the clear butter and brown milk solids sitting at the bottom. Turn up the heat slightly and brown just a little more. Then turn off the heat and allow the ghee to settle for 1–2 minutes.

Ghee

Store

CONCENTRATED SPICE PASTES

PREPARE THESE PASTES 3–4 DAYS IN ADVANCE.
PLACE IN A JAR, TOP WITH A LITTLE OIL AND REFRIGERATE. YOU CAN PLAY
AROUND WITH A LITTLE AMOUNT OF THE PASTE IN DIPS, MARINADES,
DRESSINGS AND WITH RICE OR USE TO MAKE A SUBSTANTIAL MEAT,
VEGETABLE OR PANEER DISH.

SAFFRON AND CARDAMOM PASTE

An ideal way to plan ahead for family dinners, Sunday lunch or supper with friends, or to use as an everyday condiment in other recipes.

MAKES ABOUT 250ML
PREPARATION TIME: ABOUT 30 MINUTES
COOKING TIME: ABOUT 12–15 MINUTES

FRESH

200g onions, sliced, shallow- or deep-fried until golden and crispy
3–4 garlic cloves

SPICES

seeds from 15 green cardamom pods
1 tablespoon white poppy seeds and 2–3 saffron threads, soaked in 125ml hot water for 15 minutes
1 tablespoon garam masala

PANTRY/LARDER

3 tablespoons oil
salt, to taste

NOTE
Take the seeds first, then using a mortar and pestle, grind into a fine powder.

1. Place all the above ingredients, including the soaking liquid, into a blender and grind into a smooth paste. Add a little extra oil if needed.

2. Place in a sterilised jar, seal with a tight-fitting lid and refrigerate for 5–6 days.

NOTE: Tip the whole jar into a heavy-based frying pan, fry for 30 seconds over a medium heat, then add ¼ teaspoon ground turmeric, 2 teaspoons ground cumin, 1 teaspoon red chilli flakes, then meat, paneer or vegetables of your choice, and add 50ml water. Cover and slow cook. Finish with some shredded ginger and crème fraîche or coconut milk for additional flavour.

BASIC SPICED TOMATO PASTE

It's worthwhile making a large batch, as this paste is the perfect all rounder and base for almost all Indian curries and rice dishes. No more buying jars of spice paste from supermarkets; this fresh and authentic one beats them all.

MAKES ABOUT 350ML
PREPARATION TIME: ABOUT 15 MINUTES
COOKING TIME: ABOUT 30 MINUTES

FRESH

200g onions

3–4 garlic cloves

2.5cm piece ginger, peeled

2–3 green chillies

3 bay leaves

200g tomatoes, finely diced

SPICES

3 black cardamom pods, seeds only

1 cassia or cinnamon stick

2 tablespoons coriander seeds

3 cloves

1 teaspoon ground turmeric

PANTRY/LARDER

3 tablespoons oil

salt, to taste

1. In a blender, grind the onions, garlic, ginger and chillies together to form a paste. Set aside.

2. In a coffee/spice grinder or blender, grind together all the whole spices – bay leaves, black cardamom, cassia or cinnamon stick, coriander seeds and cloves. Set aside.

3. Heat the oil in a heavy-based frying pan over a medium–high heat. Add the onion paste and fry, stirring frequently for about 5–7 minutes, or until it is a rich golden brown colour.

4. Turn the heat down slightly, add the turmeric and salt and fry for 30 seconds.

5. Next, add the tomatoes and cook until the tomatoes break down and any water has evaporated. At this stage blitz in a blender again for an even smoother paste, if you like.

6. Add the spice powder, stir and mix together well.

7. Place the paste in a sterilised jar, seal with a tight-fitting lid and refrigerate for 5–6 days.

TOPPINGS AND GARNISHES

THESE FEW ESSENTIAL INGREDIENTS CAN ADD A LITTLE EXTRA BOOST,
DRAMA AND FLAVOUR TO MOST DISHES.

CRISPY GINGER, ONION AND GARLIC

Smoky charred garlic and ginger with sweet caramelised onions. Use to garnish lentils, vegetables, meats and any rice dish.

MAKES 4–5 TABLESPOONS
PREPARATION TIME: ABOUT 5 MINUTES
COOKING TIME: ABOUT 10–12 MINUTES

FRESH
2 onions, thinly sliced
4 garlic cloves, thinly sliced
1.25cm piece ginger, peeled and finely shredded

PANTRY/LARDER
2–3 tablespoons oil
pinch of salt, or to taste

1. Heat the oil in a frying pan over a low–medium heat. Add the onions and salt, cover and cook for 2 minutes. Fry very slowly for intense flavours.

2. Remove the lid, turn up the heat slightly and add the garlic and ginger. Fry, stirring occasionally, for 5–8 minutes, or until crispy, golden but a little singed. This can be stored in an airtight container for 1–2 days, but do not place in the fridge.

TOASTED COCONUT, POMEGRANATE SEED AND CORIANDER

This has a nutty, sour and fresh flavour. Use to garnish salads, rice and dry vegetable dishes.

MAKES 2–3 TABLESPOONS
PREPARATION TIME: ABOUT 10 MINUTES

FRESH
seeds (arils) from ½ fresh pomegranate
2 tablespoons finely chopped coriander

PANTRY/LARDER
100g desiccated coconut

1. Gently toast the coconut in a non-stick pan over a low heat until golden brown, then remove and cool.

2. Mix together with the pomegranate seeds and coriander.

CURRY LEAVES, GARLIC, GINGER AND RED CHILLI

This adds an amazing South Indian flavour and heat to any dish. Use to garnish any lentil- or dhal-based dish, rice or charred and roasted vegetables.

MAKES 5–6 TABLESPOONS
PREPARATION TIME: ABOUT
8–10 MINUTES
COOKING TIME: ABOUT 2–4 MINUTES

FRESH

8 fresh curry leaves

5cm piece ginger, peeled and cut into julienne

3–4 garlic cloves, very thinly sliced

1 whole large red or green chilli, seeded (optional), and very thinly sliced

PANTRY/LARDER

2 tablespoons oil

1. Heat the oil in a small frying pan over a low–medium heat.

2. Add the curry leaves, then the ginger and fry for 20 seconds. Lower the heat slightly and add the garlic and chilli. Stir-fry until golden, crisp and slightly singed. This can be stored in an airtight container for 1–2 days, but do not place in the fridge.

MIXED NUTS AND SEEDS

This is ideal for that extra crunch and nutty flavour. Use to garnish raw salads, dips, rice and some desserts.

MAKES 5–6 TABLESPOONS
PREPARATION TIME: ABOUT 10 MINUTES
COOKING TIME: ABOUT 4–6 MINUTES

PANTRY/LARDER

85g raw cashews

85g peanuts

1 tablespoon sunflower seeds

1½ teaspoons sesame seeds

1. Preheat the oven to 160°C/315°F/Gas 2–3.

2. Place the cashews and peanuts on a baking tray and roast in the oven for 3–4 minutes, then add the seeds. Keep tossing and roast for a further 1–2 minutes.

3. Cool completely, then coarsely crush using a rolling pin or a mortar and pestle. This can be stored for approximately 2 weeks in an airtight container.

NOTE: Keep a close eye while roasting – once they go brown, they can burn very quickly.

DRY SPICE MIX

IT'S HANDY HAVING READY-MIXED SPICES – HERE ARE TWO
WONDERFUL RECIPES. ONE, A STRIPPED BACK CLASSIC FOR CURRIES
AND ALL-ROUND USE, AND THE OTHER MORE SPECIFIC IN FLAVOUR,
SO STIR INTO YOGHURT OR CRÈME FRAÎCHE AND USE AS A MARINADE,
OR ADD AT THE TAIL END OF COOKING.

KORMA MASALA

Save this one for special occasions. Mix in with cream,
yoghurt or ghee, rub over or use to marinate meat
and vegetables, then roast or barbecue.

MAKES ABOUT 2–3 TABLESPOONS
PREPARATION TIME: ABOUT 5–8 MINUTES

SPICES

8 large dried chillies, dry-roasted in a frying pan
over a gentle heat

seeds of 8 green cardamom pods

2 cinnamon sticks

1 teaspoon ground turmeric

6 cloves

1 teaspoon ground ginger

3 saffron threads

NOTE

Take the seeds from the cardamom first, then use
a mortar and pestle to grind into a fine powder.

1. Use a mortar and pestle to grind all the ingredients
into a fine powder. Place the mixture in a jar with a
tight-fitting lid and use within a month.

SIMPLE GARAM MASALA

Garam masala is the main spice mix used in almost
all Indian dishes. This is an easy version to start with.
Next, you can add further whole spices and even
dry-roast them in the oven before grinding.

MAKES 2 TABLESPOONS
PREPARATION TIME: ABOUT 5–8 MINUTES

SPICES

1 teaspoon black peppercorns

1 teaspoon cloves

5cm piece cassia or cinnamon stick

seeds of 20 green cardamom pods

seeds of 2–3 black cardamom pods

1 teaspoon cumin seeds

NOTE

Take the seeds from the cardamom first, then use
a mortar and pestle to grind into a fine powder.

1. Use a mortar and pestle to grind all the ingredients
into a powder. Place the mixture in a jar with a tight-
fitting lid and use within a month.

MARINADES

PREPARE THESE PASTES 3–4 DAYS IN ADVANCE. PLACE IN A JAR,
TOP WITH A LITTLE OIL AND REFRIGERATE. YOU CAN PLAY AROUND
WITH THE AMOUNT OF THE PASTE IN DIPS, MARINADES,
DRESSINGS AND WITH RICE, OR USE TO MAKE A SUBSTANTIAL MEAT,
VEGETABLE OR PANEER DISH.

TIKKA MASALA MARINADE

FOR CHICKEN, LAMB, PANEER AND VEGETABLES

Rich and aromatic yet a mellow marinade – it's best used on roast or barbecue chicken, fish, eggplant (aubergine), potatoes and cauliflower.

SERVES 4
PREPARATION TIME:
20 MINUTES

FRESH

340g full-fat yoghurt, preferably Greek-style style

3 garlic cloves

5-cm piece ginger, peeled

1 green chilli

SPICES

½ teaspoon ajwain seeds

2–3 saffron threads

½ teaspoon tandoori masala

½ teaspoon chilli powder

1 teaspoon garam masala

PANTRY/LARDER

1½ teaspoons white vinegar or lemon juice

½ teaspoon salt, or to taste

1 egg white

1 tablespoon oil

1. Pour the yoghurt into a large bowl.

2. In a blender, blitz the garlic, ginger and chilli together into a fine paste. Add to the yoghurt together with the rest of the ingredients, except the egg white and oil, as these need to be added just before cooking.

NOTE: During cooking, baste the meat a couple of times with melted ghee.

SPICED COCONUT AND CRÈME FRAÎCHE

FOR FISH, CHICKEN AND VEGETABLES

This marinade is best smeared over salmon steaks, a whole chicken or baby eggplant (aubergine) sliced in half and all roasted. Flake or slice any leftover salmon, chicken or eggplant, mix with good-quality mayonnaise or just a drizzle of oil, squeeze over a lime or lemon, then finish off with finely chopped spring onions and coriander. Season with coarse black pepper and sea salt. Now you have an excellent 'next day' sandwich filler.

SERVES 2–3
PREPARATION TIME:
10–15 MINUTES

FRESH

1½ garlic cloves

2 tablespoons crème fraîche

SPICES

½ teaspoon garam masala

¼ teaspoon ground turmeric

1 teaspoon chilli powder

¼ teaspoon ground black pepper

¼ teaspoon ground cumin

PANTRY/LARDER

¼ teaspoon salt, or to taste

1½ tablespoons coconut milk powder

1½ tablespoons oil

1. Begin by pounding the garlic and salt together using a mortar and pestle. Next, add all the spices and coconut milk powder to the crushed garlic and salt paste and pound together gently.

2. Slowly drizzle in the oil, and stir in until the marinade comes together and makes a thick paste.

3. Finally, stir in the crème fraîche and use immediately. Alternatively, omit the crème fraîche and pour into a sterilised jar, seal with a tight-fitting lid and refrigerate. Use within 2 days. Stir in the crème fraîche when ready to use.

MINT, CORIANDER, GINGER AND LEMON

FOR CHICKEN AND POTATOES

Rub this marinade all over whole or pieces of chicken, then cover and marinate for 2–3 hours. To add a little richness and creaminess stir in 2 tablespoons of crème fraîche or natural yoghurt to the marinade.

SERVES 4
PREPARATION TIME:
20 MINUTES

FRESH

½ bunch whole coriander

10–12 mint leaves

4cm piece ginger, peeled

3 garlic cloves

zest and juice of ½ lemon

1½ green chillies

PANTRY/LARDER

1 teaspoon salt, or to taste

1 tablespoon oil

1. Blitz all the marinade ingredients, except the oil together in a small blender. Gradually add the oil to form a paste.

2. Pour the marinade into a sterilised jar with a tight-fitting lid, refrigerate and use within 2 days.

COCONUT AND TAMARIND WITH RED CHILLI AND GROUND SPICES
FOR SEAFOOD

Marinate a whole fish in this marinade, then simply fry slivers of onion, garlic and ginger. Pop the fish including the marinade into a frying pan and fry until cooked. Alternatively, bake or barbecue with wedges of limes.

SERVES 4–6
PREPARATION TIME:
15 MINUTES

FRESH
5 tablespoons tamarind pulp
240ml tin coconut milk

SPICES
5 dried red chillies
2 tablespoons ground coriander
1 tablespoon garam masala
1½ teaspoons ground turmeric

PANTRY/LARDER
½ teaspoon salt, or to taste
3 tablespoons coconut milk powder

1. Use a mortar and pestle to pound the dried chillies into a coarse paste with 1–2 tablespoons hot water.

2. Mix the red chilli paste and tamarind pulp with the ground coriander, garam masala, turmeric and salt to taste. Add the coconut milk powder and coconut milk and mix well.

3. Pour the marinade into a sterilised jar with a tight-fitting lid, refrigerate and use within 2 days.

TAMARIND, GINGER AND CHILLI
FOR SEAFOOD AND MEAT

Rub this sour and aromatic marinade all over your choice of meat and marinate for at least a couple of hours before cooking. For a looser marinade, stir in 4–5 tablespoons coconut milk, and a large pinch of sugar, which will also help if it's too tart.

SERVES 4
PREPARATION TIME:
35 MINUTES

FRESH
10cm piece ginger, peeled and roughly chopped
2–3 chillies, roughly chopped
2 tablespoons tamarind pulp

SPICES
2 teaspoons coriander seeds
1 teaspoon mustard seeds
1 teaspoon garam masala

PANTRY/LARDER
1 teaspoon salt, or to taste
1 tablespoon oil

1. Heat a non-stick frying pan over a low heat. Roast and toss the coriander and mustard seeds for about 30–40 seconds. Cool and grind to a powder using a mortar and pestle. Set aside.

2. Next, using a mortar and pestle or a blender, grind together the ginger, chilli and 2 teaspoons hot water.

3. Then add the tamarind, roasted spices, garam masala, salt and oil and mix thoroughly.

4. Pour the marinade into a sterilised jar with a tight-fitting lid, refrigerate and use within 2 days.

SPICED YOGHURT

This marinade is delicious rubbed into a piece of chicken, beef or lamb. Stir into mixed vegetables and roast – the marinade creates its own dressing. Any leftovers can be thinly sliced and enjoyed as part of a salad or filled in any bread of your choice.

SERVES 4
PREPARATION TIME:
20 MINUTES

FRESH
500g natural yoghurt
2 garlic cloves, finely crushed
2.5cm piece ginger, peeled and finely grated

SPICES
1 tablespoon garam masala
¼ teaspoon ground turmeric

PANTRY/LARDER
3 tablespoons oil
salt and coarse black pepper . to taste

1. Stir all the marinade ingredients together and season with salt and pepper.

2. Pour the marinade into a sterilised jar with a tight-fitting lid, refrigerate and use within 1–2 days.

NOTE: During cooking, baste the meat a couple of times with melted ghee.

BOUQUET GARNI

AS AROMATIC AND ESSENTIAL AS WHOLE SPICES ARE, NOT
MANY PEOPLE APPRECIATE RANDOMLY BITING INTO THEM.
THESE LITTLE MUSLIN (CHEESECLOTH) BUNDLES HELP CONTROL AND
KEEP TRACK OF WHOLE MIXED SPICES WITHOUT COMPROMISING
ON THEIR FLAVOUR. CUT MEDIUM-SIZED SQUARES OF MUSLIN, SPREAD
OUT ON A WORK SURFACE AND PLACE THE SPICES IN THE CENTRE.
BRING THE FOUR CORNERS TOGETHER AND TIE THEM SECURELY WITH
A MEDIUM LENGTH OF KITCHEN STRING MAKING SURE THERE ARE
NO GAPS. USE IN ANY RICE, STOCK, SOUP OR MOST
SAUCE-BASED DISHES. NOTE: TRY ADDING LEMON, LIME OR ORANGE PEELS.

EIGHT WHOLE SPICE

4–5 whole black peppercorns
1 bay leaf
2–3 cloves
2–3 green cardamom pods, slightly cracked
1 black cardamom pod, slightly cracked
2 single strands of mace
1 small star anise
2.5cm piece cinnamon stick

FIVE WHOLE SPICE

4 small green cardamom pods, slightly cracked
1 teaspoon fennel seeds
4 cloves
5cm piece cinnamon stick
¼ teaspoon black peppercorns

THREE WHOLE SPICE

2.5cm piece cassia or cinnamon stick
2 bay leaves
1 teaspoon fennel seeds

FOUR WHOLE SPICE

2 cloves
1 black cardamom pod or 3 small green
cardamom pods, slightly cracked
5cm piece cassia or cinnamon stick
1 bay leaf

RICH INDIAN PASTRY

A TRADITIONAL NORTH INDIAN PASTRY – FLAKY AND BUTTERY
WITH LOTS OF FLAVOUR – IT IS A FIRM FAVOURITE AND BASE FOR
MOST INDIAN STREET SNACKS. ANY PASTRY LEFT OVER, ROLL OUT
WAFER THIN, CUT INTO STRIPS OR SHAPES OF YOUR CHOICE, SPRINKLE
WITH MIXED SEEDS, SUCH AS SESAME, CARAWAY, NIGELLA OR
BLACK POPPY SEEDS AND DEEP-FRY IN BATCHES. DRAIN AND SPRINKLE
WITH AN EQUAL SPICE MIX OF CHILLI POWDER, SEA SALT AND SUGAR.
ALTERNATIVELY, YOU CAN ADD THE SAME SEEDS TO THE DOUGH
PRIOR TO KNEADING WITH WATER.

MAKES 20–25 SAMOSAS OR PASTIES | PREPARATION TIME: 20 MINUTES

FRESH
200g butter, melted
1½ teaspoons lemon juice

PANTRY/LARDER
500g plain flour, sifted
large pinch of salt

1. Place the flour and salt in a bowl, pour in the butter and lemon juice and mix together to form breadcrumbs.

2. Using your fingertips, bind the ingredients together to form a ball, gradually adding a little warm water if necessary to bring it together into a smooth pliable dough. Cover with a damp cloth and leave for 20 minutes.

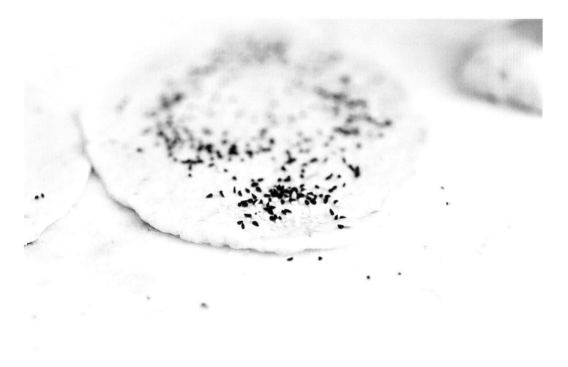

MENU IDEAS

LATE BREAKFAST AND BRUNCH: Creamy Peas and Mushrooms (p.64); Masala Scrambled Eggs (p.70); Carrot and Chickpea Pancakes (p.26); Fish, Green Beans and Spinach Kedgeree (p.22); Cardamom Coffee (p.218)

SUNDAY LUNCH: Garlic, Ginger and Chilli Prawns (p.38); Lemon and Saffron Pot Roast Chicken (p.102); Crushed Potatoes (p.156); Eggplant with Chilli and Pomegranate Dressing (p.86); Whole Spiced Fruit Salad (p.206)

AFTERNOON CHAI: Spinach and Paneer Samosa (p.52); Nargisi Egg Kofta (p.70); Fresh Tomato, Date and Tamarind Relish (p.176); Almond and Saffron Cake (p.202); Masala Chai (p.212)

WEEKDAY FAMILY DINNER: Chicken Pulao (p.152); Fresh Tomato and Curry Leaf (p.88); Kale, Chickpea, Mint and Preserved Lemon Salad (p.162); Carrot, Cucumber and Coriander Yoghurt (p.196); Chilli Hot Chocolate (p.216) (omit chillies for kids)

VEGETARIAN AFFAIR: Tarka Dhal with Spinach and Tomato (p.60); Shallots with Tamarind and Toasted Coconut (p.62); Shredded Raw Veg Salad with Spice Dressing and Nuts (p.160); Simple Plain Rice (p.134); South Indian Eggplant Pickle (p.184)

KIDS: Vegetable Parantha Rolls (p.28); Spiced Eggy Bread (p.70); Chicken Tikka Wraps (p.48); Spicy Sweet Potato Wedges (p.156); Pistachio Kulfi (p.200) (Note: just omit any chillies for kids)

LIGHT SUMMER SUPPERS: Baked Salmon (p.104); Green Beans in Tomato and Mustard Dressing (p.74); Avocado, Sweetcorn, Chilli and Coriander Salad (p.166); Fresh Lime and Lemon Soda (p.222); Pomegranate, Lime and Rosewater Granita (p.208)

CASUAL DRINKS GATHERING: Squid with Shallots, Ginger and Chilli (p.92); Sesame Seed and Ginger Chicken Skewers (p.40); Fish Fritters (p.34); Paneer and Pepper Filo Cigars (p.44); Creamy Honey and Raisin Vermicelli Pots (p.210)

INDEX

ACKNOWLEDGEMENTS

I would like to start by thanking Catie Ziller for not only commissioning me to write this book, but for believing in my ethos and direction. Hopefully this project will not only ignite an interest in cooking traditional favourites using Indian spices, but also inspire and encourage to take each spice further and be more inventive with a more relaxed attitude.

From beginning to end I have been thrilled to be able to work with my most perfect and dedicated 'dream team'. It has been mind-blowing to see the contents of my head come to life.

Thank you Lisa, your unstoppable energy is infectious, you have been so passionate and uplifting to watch – the pictures are simply stunning.

Then, Aya for being cool, calm and collected, your fresh and natural approach has truly given each dish the platform it deserves.

The backbone of Team India, Rashna for executing each page from front to back with your graceful, and extremely beautiful designs and vision – so inspiring.

Alice Chadwick, your wispy line drawings give this book an extra edge that ties the whole thing together and adds a wonderful charm.

Lovely Kathy, thank you for your patience and support during editing. It has been reassuring to know you were there.

My two gorgeous girls, Amaya Lila and Zita Rose, who have been patient, loving and always believe I can do anything. Love you both X. Also a huge and special thank you to family and friends for whom I have leant on for serious support and advice along this journey – I am eternally grateful.

Lastly, I would like to say a very special and emotional thank you to my parents, Harbhajan Singh Uppal and Sukhbinder Kaur Uppal, for without them I would know nothing. My mother, especially for her hand-held teachings of traditional North Indian cuisine and my father, for constantly inspiring me with his flamboyant, unique and innovative take on the 'spice box' and its execution. All those endless dinner parties and that experimenting in the kitchen have paid off. Both your inputs have been truly priceless.

Published in 2016 by Murdoch Books,
   an imprint of Allen & Unwin
Published by Marabout in 2016

Murdoch Books Australia
83 Alexander Street
Crows Nest NSW 2065
Phone: +61 (0) 2 8425 0100
Fax: +61 (0) 2 9906 2218
murdochbooks.com.au
info@murdochbooks.com.au

Murdoch Books UK
Ormond House
26–27 Boswell Street
London WC1N 3JZ
Phone: +44 (0) 20 8785 5995
murdochbooks.co.uk
info@murdochbooks.co.uk

For Corporate Orders & Custom Publishing, contact our Business Development Team at salesenquiries@murdochbooks.com.au.

Publisher: Corinne Roberts
Author: Amandip Uppal
Assistant Art Director: Anna Wiewiora
Main Illustrations: Alice Chadwick
Animal/Pattern Graphics: Paola Guardiani
Photographer: Lisa Linder
Food Stylist: Aya Nishimura
Editor: Kathy Steer
Production Manager: Alexandra Gonzalez

Text and design copyright © Hachette Livre (Marabout) 2016
The moral rights of the author have been asserted.

A cataloguing-in-publication entry is available from the catalogue of the National Library of Australia at nla.gov.au.

ISBN 978 1 74336 856 5 Australia
ISBN 978 1 74336 858 9 UK

A catalogue record for this book is available from the British Library.

Colour reproduction by Splitting Image Colour Studio
   Pty Ltd, Clayton, Victoria
Printed by 1010 Printing International Limited, China

IMPORTANT: Those who might be at risk from the effects of salmonella poisoning (the elderly, pregnant women, young children and those suffering from immune deficiency diseases) should consult their doctor with any concerns about eating raw eggs.
OVEN GUIDE: You may find cooking times vary depending on the oven you are using. For fan-forced ovens, as a general rule, set the oven temperature to 20°C (35°F) lower than indicated in the recipe.
MEASURES GUIDE: We have used 15 ml (3 teaspoon) tablespoon measures.